Notary Public
&
Loan Signing Agent Business

The Ultimate Insiders Guide to Launch and Scale a High-Earning Notary Side Business with Ease

Richard Walton

Table of Contents

Introduction

As businesses grow, the need for notarized documents and loan signings only increases. Venturing into this field by starting your business can offer various personal and professional advantages. In this introductory text, we will look at what is a Notary Public, the roles and responsibilities involved, and how starting your own business can lead to more significant opportunities for growth.

Overview of the Notary Public and Loan Signing Agent Business

The Notary Public and Loan Signing Agent Business is a niche industry that provides essential services to individuals, businesses, and organizations. The primary job description of a notary public is to verify the authenticity of legal documents, certify signatures, administer oaths, and witness the signing of important papers. On the other hand, loan signing agents are responsible for ensuring that all necessary paperwork related to loans or mortgages is signed accurately by all parties involved.

Becoming a notary public or loan signing agent requires specialized training and certification in most states in the US. However, once you obtain your license as a Notary Public & Loan Signing Agent professional, you can start your business quickly with low overhead costs.

This type of business offers independent professionals flexibility in working hours, allowing them to set their schedule according to client's needs while providing opportunities for personal growth through additional certifications like becoming an NSA (National Signing Agent).

Moreover, this industry provides the potential for higher income due to its unique skillset requirements, which allow you to set high rates compared with traditional jobs. Starting your own Notary Public & Loan Signing Agent Business is a great value proposition.

Definition of a Notary Public

A Notary Public is a government official who verifies the authenticity of documents and performs various legal functions. A notary can administer oaths, witness signatures, certify copies of documents and perform other duties depending on their jurisdiction.

A Notary Public's primary responsibility is to act as an unbiased observer while signing essential papers. They verify that all parties involved understand what they are signing and do so willingly without coercion or duress.

Notaries also play an essential role in preventing fraud by ensuring that signatories provide proper identification before affixing their signatures to any document. Additionally, they maintain accurate records of all notarial acts performed for future reference.

In some states, notaries can perform additional services such as loan signings or real estate closings. However, these other services require specialized training and certification beyond the basic requirements for becoming a Notary Public.

Being a Notary Public involves attention to detail, integrity, and ethical conduct. It's an essential role with significant responsibilities that help ensure the authenticity and legality of vital documents in our society.

Roles and Responsibilities of a Notary Public

A Notary Public plays a crucial role in various legal transactions. Their primary responsibility is to act as impartial witnesses while executing documents. The priority is ensuring that everyone involved in the signing process is accurately identified and fully comprehends the document's contents.

One key aspect of a Notary Public's duties consists in verifying the identity of each signing a document. It often includes checking photo identification, such as driver's licenses or passports, to confirm. It is essential to verify if a person's identity is authentic.

In addition to confirming identities, Notaries ensure that signatories enter into agreements willingly and without coercion. By doing so, they help reduce instances of fraud and protect people from potentially entering into contracts under duress.

Another vital function carried out by Notaries is administering oaths and affirmations for sworn statements or affidavits. These legal declarations hold individuals accountable for the information provided to them.

After witnessing signatures and validating identities, the notary will affix their official seal or stamp along with their signature on the document. It proves that all necessary procedures have been followed correctly during its execution process.

The Benefits of Starting Your Own Business

Starting your own Notary Public and Loan Signing Agent business can be a rewarding experience, both personally and professionally. Here are the primary benefits which you feel as a business owner.

Independence and flexibility

Starting your notary public and loan signing agent business have many benefits, including autonomy and flexibility. When you run your business, you have the liberty to make decisions about how you want to run your business. You choose what types of clients you take on, when, where to work from, the services you offer, and how much money you want to charge.

Being able to set your schedule is also a huge perk. You can decide when you should be working or taking time off without anyone telling you what's right or wrong. It allows for more balance between personal life obligations and professional responsibilities.

As an independent business owner, your income potential is unlimited. You can generate money as depend on your hard work, ability, and skill.

Starting your notary public and loan signing agent business, whether full-time or part-time basis will provide you a chance for personal growth through learning new skills such as marketing strategies or customer service techniques that help improve overall professionalism while building relationships with other professionals involved in this industry, such as real estate agents or mortgage brokers.

Potential for higher income

Starting your notary public and loan signing agent business can provide you with many opportunities, including the potential for higher income. If you run your business, earnings will depend on your many clients.

The demand for notary services is always high, especially in communities with plenty of legal and financial transactions. You can set competitive rates that align with market standards to earn more money per transaction or appointment.

Moreover, as an independent contractor, you can work on multiple assignments simultaneously, which means more revenue streams coming through. By building solid relationships with local businesses like banks and law firms - they may offer to repeat business and referrals due to trust created over time.

There are also options to expand your services by offering additional value-added benefits such as mobile notary services or specialized knowledge on niche topics within the loan signing process – thereby increasing earning potential further.

Starting a Notary Public & Loan Signing Agent Business has significant potential for higher income if strategically approached with long-term goals - it offers plenty of avenues toward professional and financial growth.

Opportunities for personal and professional growth

Starting your notary public and loan signing agent business offers financial benefits and opportunities for personal and professional development. As an entrepreneur, you'll run your own business, meaning you'll be free to make decisions that will shape your future.

One aspect of personal growth is developing new skills. By starting your own business, you'll have a chance to learn about marketing strategies, networking techniques, bookkeeping practices, and much more. You can attend workshops or training sessions to enhance your knowledge base and gain expertise in specific areas.

Another benefit of starting a notary public and loan signing agent business is professional growth. As an independent contractor, there are no limits to how far you can grow professionally. You could expand into related fields like real estate or legal services if desired.

Operating a successful notary public and loan signing agent business requires excellent customer service skills and solid written and verbal communication skills; therefore, these essential traits help hone one's overall personality development and social skills while working closely with clients from different backgrounds.

Starting a notary public & Loan Signing Agent Business offers numerous professional opportunities for those willing to take the plunge. With determination to drive education comes possibilities for long-term success in this industry by expanding skill sets through continued learning initiatives resulting in personal achievement and satisfaction while being self-employed!

How Can this Guide Help?

This guide is designed to provide valuable assistance in starting a Notary Public and Loan Signing Agent business. It offers comprehensive knowledge and information about the industry, ensuring you understand the company and its operations. By presenting detailed insights into the roles, responsibilities, and best practices of a Notary Public and Loan Signing Agent, this guide equips you with the necessary expertise to navigate the industry successfully.

Moreover, this guide provides a step-by-step approach to help you establish your business effectively. It outlines the essential steps, procedures, and considerations in setting up and running a Notary Public and Loan Signing Agent business. Whether it's obtaining the required licenses, understanding legal and regulatory frameworks, or learning about marketing strategies, this guide will serve as your roadmap, guiding you through each stage of the process.

By following the guidance presented in this guide, you can leverage the knowledge and insights to make informed decisions, avoid common pitfalls, and maximize your chances of success in the Notary Public and Loan Signing Agent business. Whether you are a starter in the industry or an experienced professional looking to start your venture, this guide will be an invaluable resource in your entrepreneurial journey.

Chapter 1

Becoming a Notary Public State by State

To serve your country as a notary public can be an excellent career. As a notary, you can witness and certify signatures on legal documents, administer oaths, and perform other essential duties. But how do you become a notary in your state? This chapter looks at becoming a notary public state by state.

What is a Notary Public?

A Notary Public is a government-appointed individual who is an impartial witness in legal transactions. They must verify the identity of individuals who sign essential documents such as deeds, wills, and powers of attorney.

The main job description of a Notary Public is to certify that the signature on a document is genuine and that all parties involved have acted voluntarily and without coercion. It helps to avoid fraud and ensure that legal proceedings are conducted fairly.

Notaries must undergo rigorous training and pass specialized exams before being licensed. They must also display strict ethical standards set forth by their state's governing body.

In addition to verifying signatures, Notaries may also administer oaths, take depositions, and perform other duties related to the law. These responsibilities vary depending on their location, area of expertise, and specific qualifications.

Becoming a Notary Public can be an excellent career choice for those who like to help others navigate complex legal processes while earning a flexible income.

The Different Types of Notary Publics

It is vital to notable that being a notary public is not a generic position. There are various types of notaries, each with distinct responsibilities and prerequisites.

One type of notary is the traditional or general-purpose notary. This type of notary can perform most functions that fall under the realm of a notary's responsibilities, such as certifying signatures and administering oaths.

Another type of notary is a mobile or traveling notary. These individuals typically go to clients' locations rather than having them come to an office. They may charge higher fees due to the convenience factor.

Some states also have electronic or e-notaries, which use technology such as digital signatures and remote video conferencing to complete transactions virtually.

Some specialized or limited-purpose notaries only perform certain transactions, like real estate closings or vehicle transfers.

Each Notary Public type has unique skills and qualifications required for performing specific tasks efficiently. Therefore, it's imperative to understand which category you belong to excel in this career path.

Pros and Cons of a Notary Public

Being a Notary Public can be an excellent source of supplemental income, offer flexible work hours and even provide networking opportunities. However, as with any job or position, becoming a Notary Public has some primary pros and cons.

One significant advantage of being a Notary Public is generating additional income. As a commissioned notary, you can charge fees for your services which typically range from $2-$15 per signature. Additionally, many businesses, such as banks or law offices, may need regular notarization services, creating consistent demand for your skills.

On the other hand, while working allows flexibility in scheduling appointments and managing time efficiently, it also means that operating costs fall on you. When using this kind of business, it's important to consider costs related to insurance coverage and complying with state regulations. These expenses should take into account.

One downside to pursuing this line of work requires extensive training and licensing procedures before receiving commission status. Furthermore, obtaining certification does mean committing time towards coursework completion, which could take several months, depending on the program chosen.

Becoming a notary public has its upsides but should only be pursued if willing to invest time into getting certified/licensed at the outset and making necessary investments in equipment/expenses required for daily operations later on down-the-line.

What States Allow You to Be a Notary Public?

Each state in the US has its set of rules and regulations for becoming a notary public. Some states have stricter policies than others, while some allow individuals with little to no experience to become a notary.

You can start your career as a notary public in several states, like Alabama, Alaska, Arizona, Arkansas, California, Colorado, Connecticut, Delaware, Florida, and Georgia. Other states that permit this profession are Hawaii, Idaho, Illinois, Indiana, Iowa, Kansas, Kentucky, Louisiana, Maine, Maryland, Massachusetts, Michigan, Minnesota, Mississippi, Missouri, Montana, Nebraska, Nevada, New Hampshire, New Jersey, New Mexico, New York, North Carolina, North Dakota, Ohio, Oklahoma, Oregon, Pennsylvania, Rhode Island, South Carolina, South Dakota, Tennessee, Texas, Utah, Vermont, Virginia, Washington, West Virginia, Wisconsin, and Wyoming.

Notably, each state has specific qualifications for becoming a notary public. You need to take an exam or complete extra training in certain situations before getting your license. It's always best practice to research the requirements in your state before embarking on any further steps towards licensure and check into any fees that might apply at initial application or renewal time.

How to be a Notary Public in Your State?

It is an excellent source of earning extra income while helping your community. To become a notary public can differ depending on the state. Can you provide more context or information? Here are some primary tips to become a notary in your state:

1. Check the requirements: Each state has policies for becoming a notary public. You may need to be legal age of 18, pass an exam, and undergo a background check.

2. Complete an application: After ensuring you meet all the relevant requirements, complete an application with your state's Secretary of State or another designated agency.

3. Pay any fees: There may be an application fee and fees for taking exams or obtaining supplies like stamps and journals.

4. Obtain training if required: Some states require completion of training courses before granting a commission as a Notary Public.

5. Take and pass any necessary exams: This will depend on your specific state's rules around testing; it could include online examinations, or in-person tests held at specified locations.

Get bonded/insured (if needed): Depending on where you live, bonding and insurance might be mandatory before being commissioned as Notary Public.

Remember that every step is vital in ensuring you become registered successfully without encountering any issues.

State-Specific Requirements and Procedures for Becoming a Notary Public

The United States has many states, and every state differs from others. It has its specific policies and procedures for becoming a notary public. As we see, some primary rules are identical in every state, like applicants must be at least 18 years, pass a background check, and complete an approved training course before submitting their application to the Secretary of State's office.

Alabama

Alabama is a state that takes the process of becoming a notary public seriously. In Alabama, you must meet these requirements, including being a legal age of 18 years old and having no felony convictions.

It is essential to become a notary public; you must first meet specific requirements. After that, you'll need to fill out an application for an appointment and submit it to the probate judge in your county of residence.

Additionally, you must provide proof of liability insurance and pay a fee for your commission.

After submitting your application, you must take an oath of office before beginning your duties as a notary public. These duties include witnessing signatures on legal documents like deeds, mortgages, and powers of attorney.

It's important to note that Alabama also allows remote online notarization (RON) by authorized electronic notaries. Alabama residents can have their documents legally signed and witnessed remotely using audio-visual technology.

Becoming a notary public in Alabama requires meeting certain qualifications and following specific steps. But with dedication and attention to detail, anyone can start their journey towards serving their community as an official witness to critical legal transactions.

Alaska

Alaska is the giant state in the USA, with unique requirements for becoming a notary public. To start your career as a notary public in Alaska, you must be a legal age of 18 years old and a state resident. It would help if you also had no felony convictions or moral turpitude offenses on your record.

After meeting the requirements, you must fill out an application and pay the Secretary of State's office a fee. In addition, you need to take an oath of office before beginning your duties as a notary public.

As an Alaskan notary public, you can perform many services, like witnessing signatures on legal documents like deeds, powers of attorney, and affidavits. However, unlike some states, there are limitations on what types of documents they can certify copies for.

Additionally, Alaska requires its Notaries Public to include specific legalese language when preparing acknowledgments or certificates stating that parties appeared before they identified themselves with satisfactory evidence, etc.

Arizona

Becoming a Notary Public in Arizona is a relatively simple process. The foremost step is to meet the eligibility requirements, which include being a legal age of 18 years old and residing in Arizona.

The next step will be about an application and paying a fee. The application includes personal information and questions about your background and education.

When your application approves, you must participate in an online course or appear in a live seminar covering Arizona's notary laws and procedures. Upon completing the system or meeting, you must clear an exam that tests your understanding of these laws and policies.

Once you clear the exam, you can officially become a notary public in Arizona. As part of this process, you must purchase a bond and obtain a seal that meets state requirements.

Becoming a notary public in Arizona is straightforward but requires careful attention to detail throughout each step of the process.

California

California, the highly populous state in America, has a great demand for public notaries. Becoming one requires completing an approved six-hour course, obtaining insurance coverage, and passing a state exam.

In California, notaries can perform acknowledgments and jurats to certify signatures on legal documents. In addition to these standard duties, they can also offer immigration consultant services if they have taken additional training.

Prospective notaries in California must understand that the application process involves submitting fingerprints for a background check conducted by the Department of Justice (DOJ) and the Federal Bureau of Investigation (FBI).

The Secretary of State regulates California's Notary Public Commission. Applicants must meet all eligibility requirements before taking required courses or exams.

Once licensed as a Notary Public in California, you may legally advertise your services if you make no false statements regarding your qualifications or abilities.

Colorado

Colorado is known for its stunning scenery, outdoor activities, and legal marijuana. But did you know that becoming a notary public in Colorado can also be a lucrative career option?

To become a notary in Colorado, one must complete an application through the Secretary of State's office. It includes submitting fingerprints, taking an oath of office, and passing an exam. Once approved, the applicant will receive their commission and can begin performing notarial acts.

Notaries in Colorado are authorized to perform various duties, including acknowledging signatures on documents, administering oaths and affirmations, and certifying copies of certain records. Legal documents must be authentic and accurate, and they rely on a crucial role played by someone to ensure their integrity.

With the growing demand for notary services in multiple industries such as real estate, finance, and healthcare, becoming a notary public in Colorado can provide financial stability and job satisfaction.

Delaware

Delaware is a state that has its own set of unique requirements for becoming a notary public. To become a notary in Delaware, you must first be a legal age of 18 years old and reside in the state. Additionally, you must never convict of a felony or any crime involving dishonesty.

To begin becoming a notary public in Delaware, you must fill out and apply to the Secretary of State's office along with your $40 fee. As a notary, it is necessary to have insurance coverage throughout your term and ensure that it remains active.

As your application approves, you will receive notification from the Secretary of State's office on when and where to go for fingerprinting. After completing this step, you must take an oath before receiving your official commission certificate.

Notably, being a notary public in Delaware comes with significant responsibility and accountability. Notaries expect to act ethically and honestly while fulfilling their witness duties during legal transactions such as document signings or oaths.

If you want to join a career as a notary public in Delaware, you must follow all necessary steps carefully while maintaining high standards of professionalism throughout your term.

Florida

Florida is one of the highly populous states in the US, and becoming a notary public here certainly has its perks. The first thing is your age should be 18 years, and a legal resident of Florida. You must also complete a course approved by the state before taking an exam.

You must submit your application, fingerprints, and proof of bonding insurance as you pass the exam. The cost may vary depending on your county, but it's around $100.

As a notary public in Florida, you can administer oaths & affirmations, witness signatures on documents such as deeds or affidavits, and certify true copies, among other duties. It's important to note that being knowledgeable about Florida's laws regarding these matters is crucial.

Becoming a notary public in Florida requires effort but can lead to fantastic opportunities for those seeking part-time work or additional income streams.

Georgia

Georgia is a state that requires a Notary Public to be commissioned by the Clerk of Superior Court in their county. The application process includes:

Applying.

Taking a training course.

Passing an exam.

Providing proof of bonding and insurance.

To become eligible for commission as a notary public in Georgia, you must be at least 18 years old and have legal residency in the United States. Additionally, you cannot have any prior felony convictions.

Once commissioned, notaries are authorized to perform several duties, such as administering oaths and affirmations and witnessing signatures on documents such as deeds or wills. They can also certify copies of official records.

Notaries are essential members of society who help prevent fraud by verifying identities and ensuring documents are signed correctly. Choosing someone trustworthy when selecting your notary public for your personal or business needs is essential.

Becoming a Notary Public in Georgia takes dedication, but ensuring essential documents are adequately witnessed and certified is worth it.

Illinois

Illinois is a state that offers its residents an opportunity to become notary publics. To have a career as a notary in Illinois, you must be at least 18, with a school diploma or equivalent. You must pass a past check and complete the required training.

The first step towards becoming a notary in Illinois is to apply to the Secretary of State's office. The application fee is $10, typically taking up to two weeks to process your application.

You must take an online training course on notarial practices and procedures as your application approves. This course covers identifying signers, maintaining records, administering oaths and affirmations, and others.

After completing the training course, you must take a written exam, which the Secretary of State's office administers. You have at least 70% on this exam to qualify for commissioning as a notary public in Illinois.

Ohio

Ohio is in the Midwest region of the United States that has specific requirements and procedures for becoming a notary public. To become a notary in Ohio, an individual must meet specific qualifications set forth by the state.

Firstly, to be eligible for appointment as an Ohio notary public, one must be at least 18 years old and have legal residency or employment within the state. Additionally, applicants must complete an approved education program offered by a provider licensed by the Secretary of State's office.

Once these requirements meet, candidates can apply to become commissioned as a notary public with their county clerk's office. The applicant must provide proof of education completion and other necessary documents such as identification and fees.

As part of maintaining their commission status, Ohio notaries have responsibilities to uphold ethical standards and follow proper procedures when performing notarial acts. These include verifying identities through personal knowledge or acceptable forms of identification and keeping accurate records of all performed actions.

Becoming a notary in Ohio requires meeting specific qualifications and following proper application procedures. As with any professional role involving legal documentation processes, responsibility and attention to detail are vital for success as an Ohio notary public.

North Carolina

North Carolina is famous for its beautiful beaches, mountains, and historic sites. If you want to have a career in a notary public in this state, there are rules and regulations which you should follow.

Firstly, you must be 18 years old and legally resident of North Carolina. You must pass a past check and have no prior criminal convictions. Next, you must complete an approved training course or self-study program before taking the notary exam.

When discussing North Carolina, you must complete a training program and pass an exam. You must submit your exam results, proof of completion, and an application form to apply. If approved, your commission will be valid for five years.

It's important to note that being commissioned as a Notary Public does not give you any additional legal authority beyond those already granted by law. Your role is to witness signatures on documents and administer oaths or affirmations.

Michigan

Michigan State is in the Great Lakes region of the United States. Becoming a notary public in Michigan involves meeting certain requirements and following specific procedures.

Like other states in Michigan, your age must be 18 years, be a resident of Michigan, or have employment that requires you to perform notarial acts within the state and pass an exam with an 80% score. Additionally, you must apply and pay the required fee.

Once your application approves and the Secretary of State's office issues your commission, you must purchase your official seal/stamp from an authorized vendor. You must also maintain records of all notarial acts performed for at least five years.

It is important to note that being commissioned as a notary public does not give you unlimited authority to perform any legal service. Notaries are only authorized to perform certain acts, such as acknowledging signatures on documents or administering oaths.

To become a licensed Notary Public in Michigan, following the proper steps and complying with all relevant laws and regulations is essential. It will enable you to serve your community with honesty and integrity.

New Jersey

If you want to serve your community, becoming a notary public in New Jersey is a great career option. To become one, you need to meet certain requirements and follow specific procedures in the state.

Firstly, applicants must be 18 years old, have no criminal record, and reside or work in New Jersey. Here, you must also complete an approved training course that includes instruction on laws related to notarial acts.

After completing the course, applicants must purchase and submit an application packet, including proof of training completion and other necessary documents such as fingerprints and fee payments. After the Secretary of State's office reviews and approves the application, candidates will notify of their approval.

New Jersey Notaries Public are authorized by law to perform various duties, including administering oaths or affirmations, taking acknowledgments or proofs of deeds and other instruments, and certifying copies. It can be a learning curve and a remarkable experience that helps strengthen communities by providing essential services like legal document verification.

Washington

If you are in Washington and want to apply for a notary public first, you will fill out the form and pay fees. Additionally, they must acquire a surety bond and purchase a notary seal to verify the authenticity of their official documents.

Becoming a notary public can open various legal, financial, or government career opportunities. Each state has specific requirements and procedures to follow to become licensed as a notary public. By understanding the steps needed for licensure in your state, you can start on the path toward this vital profession.

New York

Some specific requirements and procedures must follow in the New York notary public. First, the applicant must be at least 18 years old and a legal state resident. They must also pass an exam covering laws and regulations about notaries' public, ethical standards for notaries, and document preparation.

The applicant must submit their application and fingerprints for a background check before they can take the exam. Once approved, the applicant must purchase an official stamp or seal, including their name, county of residence, date of expiration of commission term (4 years), and other information required by law, such as their commission number.

Notaries Public in New York may legally perform acknowledgments; oaths or affirmations (jurats); certified copies thereof; affidavits; depositions or examinations under oath taken upon interrogatories submitted by any party involved in a lawsuit under Article 31 of CPLR §3118 et seq.; protests against non-acceptance or non-payment of negotiable instruments subject to objection under §3-508(2) UCC.Notary publics need to stay up-to-date with changes in laws governing them to continue providing effective services while maintaining compliance with current legislation.

By following all necessary steps outlined by New York State law when becoming a notary public, individuals can ensure they are authorized to provide valuable assistance through various means like witnessing signatures on documents and certifying copies.

Obtaining Training and Education

Obtaining training and education is the first step towards becoming a notary public. It is the primary step to know about the relevant state's rules and regulations where you want to become a notary public. The requirements for notaries vary by state, so it's vital to research your state-specific requirements before enrolling in any training programs.

Researching State-Specific Requirements

Research and comprehend your state's requirements before starting your journey to become a notary public. Each state has distinct guidelines for notaries, ranging from the qualifications required to the application process.

To research your state's requirements, visit your Secretary of State's website. You will find all relevant information regarding becoming a notary in your region. Look out for any age or residency restrictions that may apply.

It's also important to note any educational or training prerequisites that you know before applying. Some states require applicants to complete an approved course before taking their exam or submitting their application.

In addition to educational requirements, some states may have fees for obtaining a notary public commission. You will find differences per your location, so know what costs are involved beforehand.

By thoroughly understanding and researching your state-specific requirements, you'll better understand what steps to take next and how much time and effort it will take to gain this valuable certification.

Identifying Training Programs and Courses

Identifying Training Programs and Courses is crucial in your journey toward becoming a notary public. Regarding training programs, you have options ranging from online courses to in-person classroom instruction.

Before selecting a program or course, research the different providers and ensure they are reputable and recognized by your state's notary regulating agency. Some states require specific coursework or education to become a notary public, so verify that any program you choose meets those requirements.

When researching potential training programs, consider factors such as the duration of the course, schedule availability (if applicable), cost, and payment plan options. It is vital to check if the provider offers additional resources or materials to help prepare you for the exam.

Additionally, please take note of any reviews or testimonials from previous students about their experiences with the program. It can guide you into what you can expect during your training.

Identifying suitable training programs and courses requires careful consideration of various factors - but taking these steps will ultimately set you on track toward success as a notary public.

Evaluating Training Providers

Evaluating training providers is a crucial step in becoming a notary public. It involves looking at different options and determining the best value for your money.

One crucial factor to consider when evaluating training providers is their reputation. You can check the reviews from other old students.

Another option is to check the quality of their course materials. You want a provider that offers comprehensive and up-to-date information and engaging learning resources like videos, quizzes, or interactive exercises.

The delivery method of the course is another important consideration. Do you prefer online instruction, or would you instead attend in-person classes? Make sure to choose a provider that aligns with your preferred learning style.

When considering training providers, it is also essential to consider the cost. However, don't make this the deciding factor – it's worth investing more money upfront if it means a quality education will prepare you well for your role as a notary public.

The primary rule is to take your time to decide which training course suits you. How can you utilize it in a notary public career?

Enrolling in a Training Program

Enrolling in a training program is the next step after identifying suitable notary public courses and providers. Most have an enrollment process online or through phone call inquiries, but some may require personal office visits for registration.

Before enrolling, ensure you have met all prerequisites, such as age requirements and educational attainment. Some states also require background checks and references before being allowed to enroll in a course.

Once you have submitted your enrollment application, wait for confirmation from the provider regarding your admission status. It usually takes several days up to weeks, depending on the demand of the course.

It is essential to check if they offer flexible schedules that fit your daily routine without sacrificing other responsibilities or commitments. It will help if you also inquired about their refund policy if you need to back out due to unforeseen circumstances.

It's crucial to read all terms and conditions closely before signing any contract or agreement with the provider. Ensure that everything stated aligns with what discuss during initial inquiries and negotiations.

Remember that enrolling in a training program is just one part of becoming a successful notary public; dedication and hard work still need throughout your journey toward this profession.

Registration Process

After identifying the suitable training program, it's time to register for the course. The registration process may vary depending on which state you're in and which provider you've chosen. Some providers allow online registration, while others require in-person registration.

To begin with, gather all the required documents, such as proof of identity, residency, and education, before starting your registration. It keeps the process speedy and ensures that everything is ready when needed.

When registering online, follow all instructions carefully and ensure that you provide accurate information. Double-check all forms before submitting them to guarantee timely and timely enrollment.

If registering in person, make sure to arrive early enough so that there is sufficient time to complete any paperwork involved. Be prepared with questions regarding payment options or class schedules if necessary.

Taking care of these details during the registration process will help ensure a smooth transition into becoming a notary public!

Course Duration and Schedule

Before enrolling in a notary public training program, it's essential to consider the course duration and schedule. The length of the program can differ depending on the state-specific requirements and the type of training provider you choose. Some courses may require a few days, while others may take several weeks or months.

Determining how long you have available to dedicate to your notary public education is essential before selecting a course that fits your needs. Consider work schedules, family obligations, and other commitments when reviewing course schedules.

When researching potential training providers, look for programs that offer flexible and multiple options, like online classes or weekend sessions. It can help ensure you can complete your coursework within your desired time frame without interfering with other responsibilities.

Also, remember that some states require continuing education credits for public notaries even after being commissioned. Make sure to review these requirements ahead of time so that you can factor them into your overall educational timeline.

In summary, considering the duration and schedule of a notary public training program is essential to completing this process. However, with careful planning and consideration, anyone can become a skilled notary general professional!

Understanding the Exam Format

Before taking the Notary Public exam, it is vital to understand its format. The exam consists of multiple-choice questions that evaluate your knowledge of notarial laws and best practices. In every exam, you have limited time to answer these questions.

The test length varies by state, but most exams take one to three hours. Some states may require you to pass extra tests, like a written essay or an oral interview.

To ensure that you prepare for the Notary Public exam, you must familiarize yourself with its structure. It includes understanding how many questions will ask and what topics they will cover.

Notably, some states give a chance to individuals who don't pass the exam on their first attempt to retake it after a certain period has passed. However, attempts can restrict.

Knowing what to expect from the Notary Public exam can help alleviate any anxiety or stress before taking it. With proper preparation and study habits, passing this crucial test can be within reach!

Exam Preparation

Preparing for the notary public exam can be overwhelming. You can pass the exam with proper planning, hard work, and preparation.

Firstly, it is vital to familiarize yourself with the content covered in the exam. You should thoroughly review your state's notary laws and regulations, as they are crucial to the test. Studying basic legal concepts such as contracts and deeds will help you prepare.

Another helpful tip is taking practice exams. These exams are designed to mimic real-life scenarios you may encounter during your examination. They also help build confidence in your abilities before sitting for an official inquiry.

Furthermore, consider investing in study materials like books or online courses tailored explicitly towards preparing for notary public examinations. These resources provide comprehensive information about what to expect on the test and offer practical tips for passing it successfully.

Prioritizing your mental and physical health is crucial, especially during exams. Ensure you get enough rest, stay hydrated, eat nutritious meals, and exercise regularly.

Adequate preparation is vital when passing any examination - so put time aside every day leading up until test day!

Taking the Exam

Taking the Notary Exam is crucial in becoming a certified notary public. You have already prepared for this moment; it's time to deliver it perfectly.

On exam day, ensure you arrive at the testing center early with all necessary documents, including a valid ID and exam confirmation notice. It would be best if you didn't turn away due to missing documentation or needing to be on time.

Once seated and ready, take a few deep breaths to calm your nerves or anxiety. Then read through each question carefully before answering them. Take your time with the questions; take your time and double-check your answers.

Remember that some tricky questions on the exam may be designed to test your knowledge thoroughly. If you encounter such questions, don't panic! Instead, use logic and reasoning skills to work out the correct answer.

Taking an exam can be stressful, but staying focused and confident throughout will help ensure success on test day.

Receiving Exam Results

After taking the Notary Public exam, you will feel lighter. However, receiving your exam results is one more step in becoming a notary public.

The Secretary of State typically takes several weeks to grade and score exams. Once they have done so, they inform the candidates through notification by mail or email on whether they passed or failed the exam. If you pass, congratulations! You are one step closer to commissioning as a notary public.

If you do not pass, keep going. Take some time to review what areas you struggled with and focus on improving those before retaking the exam.

Once you have received passing results from the Secretary of State's office, it is time to complete any additional requirements, such as background checks and obtaining bond insurance. After completing all necessary steps and paying fees required by your state's laws, you will be commissioned as a Notary Public!

Becoming a Notary Public may seem daunting initially, but anyone can become certified with proper preparation and dedication. With this certification comes great responsibility and an opportunity to serve your community in many ways through witnessing signatures on important legal documents.

Securing a Notary Bond and Insurance

As a Notary Public, it's essential to understand the concept of notary bonds and insurance. Simply put, a notary bond is a surety bond that protects the public against any potential errors or misconduct on behalf of the notary during their duties. On the other hand, notary insurance provides additional protection for the notary and their clients.

Researching different providers for your notary bond and insurance is crucial in finding the best option. Before making a final decision, comparing prices and reading reviews from other companies that offer this service is essential.

It's easy to apply for a notary bond and insurance once you have found a provider that meets your requirements. You must provide basic personal information and proof of completing the required training courses.

After being approved for coverage by your chosen provider, paying premiums ensures that you are fully covered while performing official duties as a Notary Public. Remember that obtaining adequate protection through bonding and insurance can help protect yourself and those who rely on your services.

Understanding Notary Bond and Insurance

As a notary public, it's crucial to understand the purpose and importance of securing a notary bond and insurance.

A notary bond is an agreement between you as the notary and your bonding agency that guarantees you will fulfill your duties ethically and according to state laws. In other words, if any legal issues arise from incorrect or fraudulent actions on your part, the bonding agency will cover any damages up to the bond amount.

Notary insurance, on the other hand, provides liability coverage in case someone sues you for errors or omissions related to your notarial acts. This type of insurance can include protection against lawsuits related to identity fraud or professional misconduct.

When researching bond and insurance providers, you must choose reputable ones within the industry and have experience working with notaries specifically. Additionally, ensure you fully understand what is covered under both policies before committing to anything.

Applying for a notary bond typically involves filling out an application form where some personal information may be required, including fingerprints – depending on location requirements – which could take time but ultimately protects clients' best interests.

In summary, understanding what exactly a Notary Bond & Insurance covers is vital in protecting yourself legally in case something goes wrong while performing your duties as a Notarized.

Researching Bond and Insurance Providers

Securing a bond and insurance is crucial when becoming a notary public. But where do you start? With so many providers, how do you know which is right?

The first step in researching bond and insurance providers is to ask for recommendations from fellow notaries or business associates who have used them. You will know their reputation and level of service.

Once you have some names, take the time to research each provider online. Look at their website, read reviews on third-party websites such as Yelp or Google Reviews, and check if professional associations accredit them.

Please pay close attention to the coverage they offer. Ensure your chosen provider offers sufficient range without breaking the bank.

Remember to compare prices between different providers. It's crucial to focus on cost and ensure you're getting your money's worth.

By taking the time to research bond and insurance providers thoroughly, you can rest assured that you're making an informed decision that will protect both yourself and your clients in the future.

Applying for a Notary Bond and Insurance

After researching potential notary bond and insurance providers, it's time to apply for coverage. The application process typically involves filling out paperwork, providing personal information, and submitting any necessary documentation.

You need to prepare proper answers about your background and professional experience. Some notary bond and insurance providers may also require you to undergo a background check or credit check before granting coverage.

Select the appropriate coverage level based on your state's requirements when applying for a notary bond. You must provide proof of your bond when registering as a notary with your state's Secretary of State.

The cost of obtaining a notary bond and insurance can differ depending on several factors, such as the amount of coverage needed, the provider selected, and even geographic location. Be sure to compare pricing from different providers before making a final decision.

Once approved for bond and insurance coverage, pay all required premiums upfront to obtain complete protection against liability claims that may arise while performing your duties as a notary public.

Paying Premiums and Obtaining Coverage

Once you have chosen your provider and applied for a notary bond and insurance, the next step is to pay your premiums and obtain coverage. It's vital to understand that the cost of premiums can vary depending on several factors, such as state regulations, the type of coverage you choose, and the amount required by law.

Before paying your premium, carefully review all terms and conditions outlined in your policy. It is critical to comprehend the details of your plan, including any restrictions or exceptions that may be applicable.

After reviewing everything, if there are no issues with the terms presented by your provider, proceed to make payment. Most providers offer different payment options, like monthly or annual payments, which will depend on their policies.

Obtaining coverage once payment has been made usually takes 24-48 hours; at this point, it's crucial to check all details provided again before continuing with notarizing documents. With proper preparation beforehand when choosing a provider and understanding all aspects of one's policy contract – paying premiums becomes much more accessible while receiving adequate protection needed for work as a Notary Public.

Registering as a Notary with Your State's Secretary of State

After securing a notary bond and insurance, registering with your state's Secretary of State is the next step toward becoming a notary public. It involves submitting an application to the appropriate governing body and meeting any additional requirements for your location.

Before starting the registration process, it's essential to research your state's specific regulations and guidelines for becoming a notary. Some states may have different qualifications or require specific courses or exams before approval.

Once you've determined what is needed in your area, fill out all necessary paperwork carefully and accurately. It may include providing personal information, your bond and insurance coverage details, and relevant education or work experience.

It's also crucial to ensure all fees are paid on time and in entirety when submitting your application. Please do so to ensure processing or result in rejection.

Registering as a notary with your state's Secretary of State requires careful attention to detail and compliance with local regulations. By following these steps diligently, you can become an official notary public ready to provide valuable services within your community!

It is an excellent career to have a notary public enhance additional income or enhance your existing business. As a notary, you can provide valuable services to individuals and companies in your community while enjoying the benefits of being self-employed.

Understanding the importance of securing proper bonding and insurance is essential to become a successful notary public. You can protect yourself from potentially devastating liability issues by researching reputable providers and obtaining coverage that meets state requirements.

Additionally, registering with your state's Secretary of State office allows you to perform notarial acts within the boundaries of your jurisdiction legally. With these steps complete, you can begin marketing yourself as a reliable and professional notary public.

As always, when starting any new venture or business endeavor, research before getting started!

Chapter 2

Working as a Notary (State- By-State Requirements, Terms, and Authorized Duties)

Are you interested in the promising career of a notary public but need clarification on what the job entails or the state-by-state requirements? In this chapter, we will explore the official duties and terms of working as a notary in various states across America.

Role of a notary

We can define a notary public as a licensed professional who acts as an impartial witness when signing legal documents. Their role ensures critical legal transactions conduct honestly and authentically. Notaries' primary duty is to verify the identity of signers, administer oaths or affirmations, and certify copies of original documents.

A notary's role is to prevent fraud by confirming that all parties involved in the transaction are who they claim to be. Notaries must carefully review government-issued identification such as driver's licenses or passports to verify their authenticity.

In addition, notaries are required to maintain detailed records of each transaction they oversee. This documentation includes information about the signer's identity, the signed document type, and other relevant marketing details.

As trusted professionals within their communities, notaries must always act ethically and honestly. They must abide by strict codes of conduct and operate within state law.

Working as a notary provides individuals with both personal fulfillment and opportunities for professional growth.

Alabama

Alabama is one of the states where notaries play an essential role in adequately executing legal documents. To become a notary in Alabama, individuals must meet some special requirements set forth by the state.

Once the Secretary of State approves, Alabama notaries have several authorized duties, including administering oaths and affirmations, certifying copies of certain official documents, and executing protests for non-payment or non-acceptance of negotiable instruments such as checks or promissory notes.

Notably, while some states allow their notaries to perform marriages, this differs from duties authorized under Alabama law. Becoming an Alabama Notary Public can open up new opportunities for individuals looking to assist others with their legal documentation needs.

Alaska

Alaska is known for its vast wilderness, abundant wildlife, and stunning natural beauty. As a notary public in Alaska, you will be authorized to perform various duties, such as acknowledging signatures on legal documents and administering oaths.

It is a must for candidates that, before applying, you must complete a training course and pass an exam. It is the primary condition in Alaska.

Once approved as a notary in Alaska, you can perform various tasks like certifying copies of documents or witnessing signatures on affidavits. Notaries may also administer oaths or affirmations required by law.

As with all states, it's essential to stay up-to-date on the current notary regulations in Alaska as they change over time. Every document must handle adequately.

Arizona

Arizona is one of the US states requiring notaries to have a commission. This commission can obtain from the Secretary of State's office after completing an application and taking an exam. The application fee for a four-year term is $25, while the renewal fee is $20.

Once commissioned, Arizona notaries are authorized to perform various duties, including administering oaths and affirmations, witnessing signatures, and certifying copies of documents. In Arizona, notaries are also allowed to perform remote online notarization (RON) as long as they comply with specific requirements set by state law.

To become qualified for RON in Arizona, a notary must complete additional training on RON procedures and technology platforms approved by the Secretary of State's office. They must also obtain a surety bond worth at least $25,000 and maintain errors-and-omissions insurance coverage throughout their commission period.

Working as a notary in Arizona offers numerous opportunities for individuals looking to provide vital services within their communities or start businesses.

California

California is the highly populous state in the United States and has a significant need for notary services. To become a notary in California, individuals must clear an exam and complete a background check. Notaries in California have several authorized duties, including administering oaths and affirmations, taking acknowledgments, certifying copies of documents, and more.

One important thing to note about being a notary in California is that it is unlawful to offer legal advice or provide assistance with immigration paperwork unless you are an attorney licensed by the State Bar of California. Additionally, notaries cannot prepare legal documents or represent others.

In California, notaries must keep records of official acts, such as journal entries, and maintain a bond of at least $15,000 during their commission term. It's also worth noting that certain restrictions exist on what types of documents can be certified by a notary public in California.

Becoming a notary public in California requires passing rigorous exams and adhering to strict guidelines set forth by the state. But those who do meet these requirements can play an essential role in assisting Californians with various legal transactions.

Colorado

Becoming a notary public in Colorado is a straightforward process. You should complete and submit a form to the Secretary of State's office. It's important to note that a notary must be a fluent English reader, writer, and state resident.

Once approved, notaries in Colorado can perform various authorized duties, including administering oaths and affirmations, certifying copies of documents, and witnessing signatures on legal documents like deeds and wills. Additionally, they can approve vehicle identification numbers (VIN) for buyers who want to register their vehicles.

Colorado notaries must also maintain accurate records of all their official acts. These records should include information about the date and time each action was performed and details about any fees charged.

Only authorized persons may access these records to prevent fraud or misconduct by Colorado notaries while performing their duties properly.

Delaware

Delaware, known as "The First State," has specific requirements for becoming a notary. To become a Delaware notary, you must be 18 years old and reside or work there. You must also complete an application process, including fingerprinting and a background check.

Once licensed, notaries in Delaware can perform acknowledgments, take depositions, certify copies of documents, and administer oaths. However, unlike some states where notaries have broad powers to perform marriages or solemnize oaths of office, Delaware does not authorize these duties.

Delaware has strict rules about proper identification when signing documents before a notary. Acceptable forms of ID include driver's licenses issued by any state, U.

S. passports, military IDs, or other government-issued photo identification cards.

In addition to their authorized duties as public officials, Delaware's Notaries Public are held responsible for understanding their legal obligations and avoiding impropriety in performing their official acts as Notary Public.

Florida

Becoming a notary public is a significant responsibility but also a rewarding vocation. Each state has its requirements and terms of service, so it's essential to research the regulations in your jurisdiction.

Knowledge of a notary's official duties will help you provide exceptional services to clients who require authentication for legal documents.

Whether you seek to become a notary or need one for personal or professional purposes, don't hesitate to reach out and find one within your state's guidelines. A competent notary can make all the difference in ensuring that legal documents are valid and legally binding.

Georgia

The state's Secretary of State appoints Georgia notaries public. He should have a grip on English to read and write.

Once appointed, Georgia notaries have several authorized duties they may perform. These include administering oaths and affirmations, taking acknowledgments and verifications, witnessing signatures on documents such as deeds or wills, certifying copies of certain records or documents, and issuing protests.

Marriage officiation is absent from this list; unlike other states where notaries can legally marry couples, Georgia does not permit its notaries to do so. Additionally, while Georgia notaries can perform remote online notarization (RON), there are strict rules governing how this process may take place.

Working as a notary in Georgia is fruitful. You are not only serving society, but also you ca generate extra income.

Illinois

Illinois state is situated in the Midwestern region of the United States. Illinois has specific requirements for interested candidates that must be fulfilled. A notary resides or works within the state.

Further, applicants must complete an approved course of study and pass an examination before receiving their commission. The application fee for a notary public commission is $10.

Once commissioned, notaries in Illinois have several authorized duties, including administering oaths and affirmations, taking acknowledgments and proofs of written instruments, certifying copies of documents, and witnessing document signatures.

Notaries also have certain limitations on their authority, such as being prohibited from giving legal advice or performing any acts that constitute the unauthorized practice of law. It's essential for Illinois notaries to always stay up-to-date with changes to state laws regarding their duties and responsibilities.

Becoming a notary public in Illinois requires meeting specific eligibility criteria, completing necessary education requirements, and passing an exam.

Ohio

Ohio is a state that requires notaries to be commissioned by the Secretary of State. To become a notary in Ohio, applicants must meet specific requirements, such as being at least 18 years old and living in Ohio or working within the state.

Once appointed, notaries can perform various authorized duties such as administering oaths, taking acknowledgments and affirmations, and certifying copies of documents. Notaries are also able to act as witnesses for signatures.

Ohio notaries need to keep accurate records of all transactions they perform. The state requires notaries to maintain an official journal where they record information about each transaction, including the date, type of document, name of the signer, and any other pertinent details.

Additionally, Ohio law allows electronic signatures on documents but only if it meets specific criteria outlined by the Secretary of State's office. Notaries may also use electronic seals when performing their duties.

Becoming a notary in Ohio requires meeting certain qualifications and following specific guidelines set forth by the state government. But with proper training and attention to detail, individuals can provide valuable services as trusted public official.

North Carolina

North Carolina requires notaries to undergo training and pass a written examination before being commissioned. The North Carolina Secretary of State's office handles notary commissioning, and applicants must meet specific requirements before being eligible for commissioning.

To become eligible, one must either reside or work within the state, finish an accredited course of study, successfully pass an examination provided by the Secretary of State's office, and file an application with the necessary fees.

Once commissioned, North Carolina notaries are authorized to perform various duties, such as acknowledging signatures on documents like deeds and powers of attorney. They can also administer oaths or affirmations when necessary.

Moreover, North Carolina notaries must follow specific guidelines when performing their duties. For example, they should ensure that signers understand the content of any document they are signing and confirm signers' identities through proper identification methods.

Becoming a notary public in North Carolina requires passing a rigorous process that ensures only qualified individuals practice as Notaries Public. Once appointed as Notaries Public in this great state, several official acts are entrusted to these officials, which should carry out according to strict rules governing their conduct.

Michigan

Michigan is a state requiring notary applicants to undergo a training course and pass an exam. The state also requires a background check, fingerprinting, proof of insurance coverage, and a $10,000 surety bond.

Once licensed as a Michigan Notary Public, you can witness signatures on legal documents like deeds, wills, legal documents, and powers of attorney. You can also administer oaths and affirmations.

In Michigan, there are certain restrictions for notaries. For example, you can only offer legal advice or prepare legal documents if you're an attorney licensed in the state. Additionally, if your employer is interested in notarizing the transaction - directly or indirectly – you cannot serve as the notary.

It's important to note that Michigan does allow remote online notarization (RON) under specific guidelines, which will enable signers from different locations within the USA or even abroad to be able to have their document signed by a MI Notary without having physically present at the signing location, thus saving time and travel expenses while ensuring security measures are met during virtual meetings with clients.

New Jersey

If you are passionate about becoming a notary public in New Jersey, it is vital to understand the various prerequisites and regulations involved.

Individuals wishing to obtain a notary commission must complete the form and pay the required fee. The application will require personal details, employment history, and criminal background checks.

Once approved, New Jersey notaries have several authorized duties, which include administering oaths and affirmations; taking acknowledgments of deeds or other instruments; witnessing signatures on documents; certifying copies of documents; and protesting negotiable instruments.

Moreover, it's essential to note that all official notarial acts in NJ must use either an inked rubber stamp seal or an embossed seal. Notaries must also keep a journal record book of every official action performed.

Being a notary public in New Jersey requires diligence and attention to detail but can offer many opportunities for those who seek them out.

Washington

When we see the requirements in Washington, to become a notary, you need to meet specific conditions such as 18 years old with no felony convictions or disqualifying criminal histories. Secondly, you must complete a training course and pass the state's notary exam.

Once you are commissioned as a notary public in Washington, your authorized duties include:

Administering oaths and affirmations.

Taking acknowledgments.

Witnessing signatures on affidavits, depositions, or other documents.

Certifying copies of records.

Issuing protests related to non-payment or dishonor of negotiable instruments.

Performing any other acts permitted by law.

Washington State requires its notaries public to renew their commissions every four years. To do so, they must retake the exam and satisfy any continuing education requirements set forth by the Secretary of State's office.

New York

Notaries in New York are authorized to administer oaths and affirmations and take acknowledgments and witness signatures. They also have the power to certify copies of certain documents. You must be a state resident or have a physical office or business location within the state's boundaries.

Becoming a notary differs from state to state, and the requirements and duties also vary. Nonetheless, being a notary can be a rewarding experience because it enables you to assist your community by certifying critical legal documents. If you're intrigued by this profession and meet the prerequisites for becoming a perfect notary public in your state, pursue it. You won't be disappointed.

Notary Public Terms and Definitions

As with any profession, working as a notary public comes with its terms and definitions. Understanding these terms is essential to communicate with clients and colleagues effectively.

One of the most common phrases you'll come across is "notarization." It refers to the act of verifying that a signature on a document is authentic. Notaries are authorized by their state government to perform this service.

Another term you'll hear often is "acknowledgment." An acknowledgment is when an individual declares to a notary public that they signed a document voluntarily and without coercion.

A third term worth noting is "jurat." A jurat requires an individual to swear under oath or affirm that the contents of a document are true and accurate.

It's also essential for notaries public to be familiar with identification documents such as driver's licenses, passports, and other forms of ID. These documents help verify the identity of signers before performing notarial acts.

Understanding these basic terms will give you the foundation to excel as a notary public.

Authorized Duties of a Notary Public

As a Notary Public, there are specific duties that you're authorized to perform. The most significant responsibility is verifying the identity of individuals signing legal documents and administering oaths.

In addition to identifying signers, notaries can also witness signatures and certify copies of essential records such as birth certificates or passports.

Notaries may also be called upon to handle loan signings, which involve reviewing and verifying the accuracy of loan documents before borrowers sign them. This responsibility requires attention to detail since even minor errors can have significant consequences for all parties involved.

Notaries must understand their limitations when it comes to providing legal advice or performing tasks outside their scope of practice. Doing so could result in serious ethical violations or even legal action against them.

Notaries are essential in ensuring the legality and validity of crucial documents while always upholding a high standard of professionalism.

Notary Public Ethics and Professionalism

As a Notary Public, conducting oneself with the highest level of ethics and professionalism is essential. These characteristics are critical in ensuring that all notarial acts are performed accurately, impartially, and honestly.

One of the most crucial ethical considerations for Notaries Public is maintaining impartiality when performing notarial acts. A Notary must be unbiased when witnessing signatures or verifying identities to avoid conflict of interest.

Another key aspect of being a professional Notary Public is maintaining confidentiality. All information obtained during the performance of notarial acts must remain confidential unless required by law or court order.

A professional approach also includes correctly identifying signers and keeping accurate records. The identification process verifies the signer's identity, and recordkeeping accurately documents all actions.

Furthermore, Notaries must keep up-to-date on laws affecting their profession and seek expert advice if they need help with specific situations. Ultimately, adhering to high standards of integrity helps maintain public trust in both individual Notaries and the institution.

Notary Public Liability and Errors and Omissions Insurance

As a notary public, your primary duty is to verify the identity of signers and prevent the public from fraud. You ensure that they understand the contents of the documents they are signing. It seems an easy task; it is not; mistakes can happen. Having errors and omissions insurance is a must to prevent mistakes.

E&O insurance safeguards notaries against financial losses caused by claims made against them for any negligent acts, errors, or omissions committed while performing their duties as a notary public. This type of insurance covers legal fees, damages awarded by a court, and settlements.

If a notary makes a mistake or leaves something out while performing their official duties, they can be held responsible if someone is harmed. It is known as notary public liability. The person who faced injury has the right to sue for compensation for any damage caused by improper execution or handling of documents.

Without E&O insurance coverage, these types of lawsuits can be financially devastating to notaries – especially those who work independently without any employer-provided coverage. Therefore, every practicing notary must obtain an adequate amount of E&O insurance coverage on their own.

As a notary public, it is crucial to understand the importance of liability insurance, specifically Errors and Omissions (E&O) insurance. Notary public liability insurance provides coverage for potential errors, mistakes, or omissions made during the notarization process. Let's explore this topic further.

1. Understanding Notary Public Liability:

As a notary public, you are responsible for verifying the authenticity of signatures, ensuring the legality of documents, and preventing fraud. However, mistakes or errors can occur, which may result in financial losses or legal consequences for your clients. Notary public liability insurance protects you in the event that a client alleges you made an error or acted negligently during the notarization process.

2. Importance of Errors and Omissions Insurance:

Errors and Omissions insurance, also known as professional liability insurance, is a specific type of coverage that protects professionals, including notaries, from claims of negligence, errors, or omissions in their services. E&O insurance is crucial because even the most diligent notaries can make mistakes, and these mistakes can have serious consequences. Having E&O insurance helps safeguard your business and personal assets in case of a lawsuit arising from a client's financial loss or damages resulting from an error or omission.

3. Coverage Provided by E&O Insurance:

Errors and Omissions insurance typically covers legal defense costs, settlements, and judgments arising from claims related to your notarial acts. This includes errors in document preparation, incorrect identification of signers, failure to administer oaths properly, or any other mistakes made during the notarization process. E&O insurance provides financial protection, helping to cover legal fees and potential damages, ensuring that your personal assets are not at risk.

4. Coverage Limits and Deductibles:

When obtaining E&O insurance, it is important to understand the coverage limits and deductibles associated with the policy. Coverage limits refer to the maximum amount the insurance company will pay for a claim. Deductibles are the out-of-pocket expenses you are responsible for paying before the insurance coverage kicks in. It is crucial to select coverage limits and deductibles that align with your business needs and risk tolerance.

5. Professional Conduct and E&O Insurance:

While E&O insurance provides financial protection, it is essential to maintain professional conduct and adhere to the highest standards of notarial practice. Continuously strive to improve your skills and stay updated on laws and regulations relevant to your profession. Diligently following proper procedures and exercising caution can help minimize the risk of errors and claims. E&O insurance should not be seen as a substitute for competent and ethical notarial practice but rather as an additional layer of protection.

6. Obtaining Notary Public Liability Insurance:

To obtain notary public liability insurance, contact insurance providers that specialize in professional liability coverage for notaries. Research different insurance companies, compare coverage options, and obtain quotes to find the policy that best suits your needs. Consider factors such as coverage limits, deductibles, policy exclusions, and the reputation and financial stability of the insurance provider.

7. Maintaining Insurance Coverage:

Once you have obtained notary public liability insurance, it is important to maintain continuous coverage. Keep your policy active and pay your premiums on time to ensure uninterrupted protection. Review your policy periodically to ensure that it still meets your coverage needs and make adjustments as necessary.

8. Disclosing Insurance Coverage to Clients:

To instill confidence in your clients and demonstrate your commitment to professionalism, it is advisable to disclose your notary public liability insurance coverage. Including a statement on your website or in your business communications can reassure clients that you are prepared for any potential errors or omissions and that their interests are protected.

Notary public liability and Errors and Omissions insurance provide essential protection for notaries in the event of errors, mistakes, or omissions made during the notarization process. Obtaining appropriate insurance coverage can help safeguard your business and personal assets, providing financial protection in case of claims or lawsuits. While insurance is important, it should always be complemented by adherence to best practices, continuous professional development, and ethical notarial conduct. By understanding the importance of liability insurance and obtaining suitable coverage, you can mitigate potential risks and ensure the long-term success of your notary business.

Notary Public Recordkeeping and Journal Entries

As a Notary Public, keeping records of all notarial acts performed is essential. It is why keeping an accurate journal entry is crucial for recordkeeping purposes.

The journal entry should include the date, time, location, document type notarized, signer(s) name, and any other relevant details about the transaction. Including a thumbprint in the journal entry is also recommended as an added security measure.

It's vital to note that each state has specific rules regarding how long journals must keep and when they can dispose of. Notaries must stay current on their state's regulations and requirements.

In addition to recording notarial acts in a journal, Notaries are required by law to maintain copies of any documents they notarize. These copies should be stored safely and securely for future reference if needed.

By staying organized with proper recordkeeping practices like these, Notaries can ensure accuracy in their work while protecting themselves from potential liability issues.

As a notary public, maintaining accurate recordkeeping is a critical aspect of your role. Keeping detailed records and journal entries is essential for demonstrating compliance with laws and regulations, protecting yourself from liability, and ensuring the integrity of the notarial process. Let's explore this topic further.

1. Importance of Recordkeeping:

Recordkeeping serves several purposes in notarial practice. It provides a historical record of the notarization, establishes a chain of custody for important documents, and acts as evidence of the notarial act performed. Additionally, recordkeeping helps you maintain accountability and transparency, ensuring that you are fulfilling your obligations as a notary public.

2. Required Notary Journal:

In many jurisdictions, notaries are required by law to maintain a notary journal or record book. The journal serves as an official log of all notarial acts performed. It captures crucial information about each transaction, including the date, time, type of notarial act, names and signatures of the parties involved, identification details, and any fees charged. Check the regulations specific to your jurisdiction to ensure compliance with journaling requirements.

3. Detailed Journal Entries:

Each entry in the notary journal should be detailed and complete. Include all the necessary information to document the notarization accurately. This includes the type of document notarized, any additional documents involved, the purpose of the notarization, and any special circumstances or requirements. Record any identification presented, such as driver's licenses or passports, including the identification number, issuing authority, and expiration date. Additionally, note any witnesses present and their identification details, if applicable.

4. Timely and Sequential Entries:

Make it a practice to record journal entries immediately after performing a notarial act. Timely entries help ensure accuracy and prevent any confusion or omission of important details. It is essential to maintain a sequential order of entries in the journal, as this helps establish a clear and consistent record of notarial acts performed over time.

5. Consistency and Neatness:

Maintain consistency and neatness in your journal entries. Use legible handwriting or consider using a computerized journaling system if permitted by your jurisdiction. Make sure entries are clear, organized, and easy to understand. Avoid using abbreviations or jargon that may cause confusion or ambiguity.

6. Secure Storage of Journal:

The notary journal is a legal record and must be securely stored to protect its integrity and confidentiality. Keep your journal in a safe and secure location, such as a locked cabinet or safe, to prevent unauthorized access. Treat the journal as confidential and refrain from sharing its contents with anyone other than authorized individuals, such as law enforcement or regulatory agencies, if required by law.

7. Retention Period:

Different jurisdictions have specific requirements for how long notary journals must be retained. Familiarize yourself with the retention period mandated by your jurisdiction and ensure compliance. Some jurisdictions require notary journals to be retained for several years after the last entry, while others may have different retention periods. Properly archiving and storing old journals is crucial for maintaining compliance with recordkeeping regulations.

8. Use of Technology for Recordkeeping:

With advancements in technology, some jurisdictions allow notaries to keep electronic records instead of physical journals. Electronic notary journals can provide added convenience, efficiency, and security. If electronic journaling is permitted in your jurisdiction, research and choose a reliable electronic journaling system that meets all legal requirements and ensures the integrity and confidentiality of the records.

9. Reviewing and Auditing Journal Entries:

Regularly review your notary journal entries to ensure accuracy and completeness. This helps identify any errors or discrepancies that may need to be corrected. Performing periodic self-audits of your journal entries can help maintain the integrity of your records and ensure compliance with applicable laws and regulations.

10. Legal and Professional Obligations:

As a notary public, it is your legal and professional obligation to maintain accurate and complete records. Failure to keep proper records or maintain a journal may result in legal consequences or disciplinary action. By prioritizing recordkeeping and journal entries, you demonstrate your commitment to upholding the integrity of the notarial process and providing reliable services to your clients.

Maintaining detailed recordkeeping and journal entries is essential for notaries public. Accurate and complete records help demonstrate compliance, protect against liability, and preserve the integrity of notarial acts. Adhere to the recordkeeping requirements specific to your jurisdiction, maintain consistency and neatness in your entries, and securely store your journal. Regularly review and audit your journal entries to ensure accuracy and compliance. By fulfilling your recordkeeping obligations, you enhance professionalism, instill confidence in your clients, and contribute to the integrity of the notarial profession.

Notary Public Regulations and Changes in the Digital Age

Notary public regulations have evolved, and with the advent of technology in the digital age, changes have been made to adapt to these new advancements. Many states have implemented electronic notarization into their laws in response to the increasing need for remote notarization.

Electronic notarization is a process that allows documents to be signed and sealed electronically by a notary public. This process eliminates the need for physical presence at an office or location, allowing individuals worldwide to access this service remotely.

However, while electronic notarization has its benefits, it also poses unique challenges, such as establishing identity verification through virtual means. Some states require additional measures such as video conferencing or biometric authentication to overcome the challenge.

Another change in regulations is related to recordkeeping and journal entries. With electronic signatures becoming more prevalent today, it has become necessary for notaries public to maintain digital records of all transactions conducted during each appointment.

Regulation changes are required due to technological advancements affecting every industry; therefore, adjustments must be made within the legal system. Adopting electronic signature tools reduces turnaround times significantly without compromising on security levels but also requires proper identification procedures to maintain their standards of professionalism at all times.

In the digital age, notary public regulations have undergone significant changes to accommodate technological advancements and evolving business practices. As technology continues to transform the way we conduct business and handle documents, let's explore how notary public regulations have adapted to these changes.

1. Electronic Signatures and Digital Documents:

One of the most significant changes in the digital age is the acceptance of electronic signatures and digital documents. Many jurisdictions now recognize the validity and enforceability of electronic signatures, which has opened up new possibilities for notarial acts conducted online. Notaries can now notarize digital documents remotely, eliminating the need for physical presence and streamlining the notarization process.

2. Remote Online Notarization (RON):

Remote Online Notarization (RON) is a practice that allows notaries to perform notarial acts remotely using audio-visual technology and secure digital platforms. RON has gained traction in many jurisdictions as a convenient and efficient way to notarize documents from anywhere, at any time. Notaries must comply with specific regulations and requirements to perform RON, including using approved technology platforms and implementing appropriate security measures to protect the integrity of the notarization process.

3. Legal Recognition and Standards:

Regulatory bodies and legislative authorities have recognized the need to update notary public regulations to accommodate digital practices. Many jurisdictions have enacted laws and regulations that specifically address electronic signatures, digital documents, and remote notarization. These regulations outline the requirements for electronic notarization, prescribe security measures, and establish standards for technology platforms used in remote notarization.

4. Identification and Identity Verification:

Identity verification is a fundamental aspect of notarial acts. In the digital age, notaries must adopt robust procedures to verify the identity of signers in remote notarization scenarios. Various digital identity verification methods, such as knowledge-based authentication, biometric verification, and multi-factor authentication, are being implemented to ensure the integrity and security of the notarial process.

5. Security and Data Privacy:

With the digital transmission and storage of documents, notaries must prioritize security and data privacy. Regulations often require notaries to use secure technology platforms that protect sensitive information and ensure the confidentiality of client data. Notaries must also comply with data protection laws and implement appropriate security measures to prevent unauthorized access, data breaches, and identity theft.

6. Training and Certification:

The digital age has necessitated training and certification programs to equip notaries with the knowledge and skills required for electronic notarization. Notaries may need to undergo specialized training on electronic signatures, digital document handling, remote notarization procedures, and technology platforms. Certification programs and continuing education courses provide notaries with the necessary expertise to adapt to changing regulations and effectively perform their duties in the digital realm.

7. Jurisdictional Variances:

Notary public regulations and requirements can vary from jurisdiction to jurisdiction. While many jurisdictions have adopted electronic and remote notarization practices, there may still be variations in the specific rules and processes. Notaries should stay informed about the regulations applicable in their jurisdiction and comply with any specific requirements for electronic notarization.

8. Ongoing Adaptation and Evolution:

Notary public regulations in the digital age are not static. They continue to evolve as technology advances and new challenges arise. Regulatory bodies and professional associations are actively engaged in monitoring industry trends, assessing the impact of technology, and updating regulations to ensure that notary public practices remain secure, reliable, and aligned with legal requirements.

Notary public regulations have adapted to the digital age by recognizing electronic signatures, digital documents, and remote notarization practices. The acceptance of electronic signatures and the emergence of remote online notarization have revolutionized the way notaries operate. Notaries must stay informed about the regulations in their jurisdiction, adhere to identity verification and security standards, and undergo specialized training to perform electronic notarization effectively. As technology continues to evolve, notary public regulations will likely continue to adapt to meet the changing needs of the digital landscape.

Notary Public Associations and Resources

As a notary public, staying current with industry changes and regulations is essential. One option to do this is by joining a notary public association. These associations offer valuable resources, networking opportunities, and continuing education courses.

The National Notary Association (NNA) is one of the largest organizations for notaries in the United States. They offer various resources, including training videos, webinars, and articles on topics ranging from identity theft prevention to best practices for remote online notarization.

Another notable organization is the American Society of Notaries (ASN). ASN offers its members educational materials such as handbooks, newsletters, and liability insurance coverage.

In addition to these national organizations, state-specific associations are often available for notaries. These groups can provide localized information on regulations and networking opportunities with fellow professionals in your area.

Becoming involved in a notary public association can be incredibly beneficial for staying informed about industry updates and connecting with other professionals in the field.

Working as a notary public is an important job that requires attention to detail, professionalism, and ethical behavior. Notaries must know their authorized duties and maintain accurate recordkeeping practices, including journal entries for every notarization performed. Liability insurance is also essential to protect against errors and omissions.

As technology advances, regulations surrounding notary publics are also evolving. Notaries must stay updated with changes in the digital age and utilize resources available through associations such as the National Notary Association or the American Society of Notaries.

If you like aiding others with vital legal documents and ensuring they are precise and compliant with state laws, becoming a notary public could be a worthwhile career option. By following proper procedures and maintaining high standards of professionalism, one can build a successful business in this field.

Chapter 3

Starting a Loan Signing Agent Business

Have you considered becoming a loan signing agent? As the demand for mortgage loans continues to rise, so does the need for skilled professionals to facilitate smooth loan closings. That's where loan signing agents come in! In this chapter, we'll explore everything you need to know about starting your own loan signing agent business - from understanding the role and responsibilities of a loan signing agent to the essential tools and equipment required for success.

Starting a loan signing agent business can be a lucrative venture for notaries looking to expand their services and increase their earning potential. Loan signing agents play a vital role in the mortgage industry by facilitating the signing and notarization of loan documents. Here are some key aspects to consider when starting a loan signing agent business:

1. Obtain the Necessary Education and Training:

To become a successful loan signing agent, it is important to acquire the necessary education and training. Familiarize yourself with the loan documents involved in various types of mortgage transactions, such as purchase loans, refinance loans, and home equity loans. Attend training programs specifically designed for loan signing agents to gain a comprehensive understanding of the loan signing process, borrower interactions, and the notarial acts involved.

2. Obtain Proper Certification:

While not all jurisdictions require specific certification to become a loan signing agent, obtaining certification can enhance your credibility and marketability. Several organizations offer loan signing agent certification programs that provide in-depth training and assessments to ensure you have the necessary knowledge and skills to perform the job effectively. Certification can also help you establish professional connections and gain access to signing service platforms.

3. Establish Relationships with Signing Services:

Signing services act as intermediaries between loan signing agents and mortgage lenders or title companies. Building relationships with signing services can provide a steady stream of assignments and clients. Research reputable signing services in your area and submit your credentials to be considered for assignments. Networking with other notaries and industry professionals can also help you establish connections and gain referrals.

4. Market Your Services:

Effective marketing is essential for attracting clients and growing your loan signing agent business. Create a professional website that showcases your services, credentials, and contact information. Utilize social media platforms to engage with potential clients and share relevant industry updates. Consider joining professional organizations and attending industry events to network with mortgage professionals and expand your business reach.

5. Develop a Professional Image:

As a loan signing agent, presenting a professional image is crucial. Dress appropriately when meeting clients and conducting signings, as it helps instill confidence and trust. Have a well-organized and mobile office setup, including a reliable laptop or tablet, printer, scanner, and necessary notary supplies. Maintain a high level of professionalism in all your interactions and communications with clients, ensuring a positive and efficient signing experience.

6. Understand Loan Documents:

Loan signing agents must have a solid understanding of various loan documents, including promissory notes, deed of trust, mortgage agreements, and disclosure forms. Familiarize yourself with the content and purpose of each document to guide borrowers through the signing process confidently. Stay updated on changes in loan documents and industry regulations to provide accurate information to clients.

7. Build a Network of Professionals:

Developing relationships with professionals in the mortgage industry can benefit your loan signing agent business. Connect with real estate agents, mortgage brokers, and title companies to establish referral partnerships. Attending local industry events and joining professional associations can provide opportunities to network and build a reliable network of industry contacts.

8. Provide Excellent Customer Service:

Delivering exceptional customer service is crucial in the loan signing agent business. Be responsive, reliable, and professional in all your interactions with borrowers, signing services, and other industry professionals. Ensure that the signing process is smooth and efficient, answering any questions or concerns the borrower may have. Going the extra mile to provide a positive experience can lead to repeat business and referrals.

9. Stay Updated on Industry Changes:

The mortgage industry is dynamic, with regulations and practices that can evolve over time. Stay informed about industry changes, updates in loan signing procedures, and any legal or regulatory requirements that may impact your business. Attend continuing education courses, join industry forums, and read industry publications to stay up to date with the latest developments.

Starting a loan signing agent business requires a combination of knowledge, skills, and a proactive approach to marketing and client acquisition. By focusing on professionalism, continuous education, networking, and excellent customer service, you can establish a successful and profitable loan signing agent business.

Importance of loan signing agents in the mortgage industry

The mortgage industry is a complex network of players, from lenders to borrowers, real estate agents, and title companies. Amidst all this chaos lies an important role - that of the loan signing agent. Indeed, these professionals are crucial in ensuring that loan documents are accurately signed and delivered for processing.

These individuals have become valuable because they bridge the gap between clients needing loans and financial institutions providing them. With loan signing agents, navigating the various legal processes involved in taking out a mortgage or other types of loans would be easier.

Moreover, with more people turning to online platforms for their banking needs due to COVID-19 pandemic restrictions on physical interactions, professional loan signing agents have become increasingly vital. They can ensure easy access while maintaining high confidentiality and accuracy in document handling.

Loan signing agents are indispensable figures in the mortgage industry, playing a pivotal role in facilitating the seamless execution of loan documents and ensuring compliance with legal requirements. Their expertise and proficiency in navigating the intricacies of the mortgage signing process make them vital assets for lenders, borrowers, and all parties involved in the transaction.

In today's complex mortgage landscape, loan signing agents bring a wealth of knowledge and experience to the table. They possess a deep understanding of the diverse range of loan documents encountered in different mortgage transactions, including purchase loans, refinance loans, and home equity loans. This expertise allows them to guide borrowers through the labyrinthine world of mortgage paperwork, ensuring that they fully comprehend the terms, conditions, and implications of their loan agreements before appending their signatures.

Moreover, loan signing agents serve as conduits of legal compliance. They bear the responsibility of verifying the identities of borrowers and ensuring that all notarial acts are conducted in strict adherence to the prevailing legal standards and regulations governing their jurisdiction. By meticulously adhering to these guidelines, loan signing agents safeguard the interests of all stakeholders involved, ensuring the legitimacy and enforceability of loan documents.

Efficiency and accuracy are paramount in the mortgage industry, and loan signing agents excel in these domains. They act as orchestrators, expertly coordinating with borrowers, lenders, and other involved parties to orchestrate the timely and seamless execution of loan documents. Through their astute organization and meticulous attention to detail, loan signing agents minimize delays and errors, enabling mortgage transactions to progress smoothly and efficiently.

The utilization of loan signing agents also brings about significant time and cost savings for both lenders and borrowers. By providing mobile services, loan signing agents eliminate the need for borrowers to undertake arduous journeys to lenders' offices. Instead, signings can occur at the borrower's preferred location, whether it be their home, workplace, or any mutually convenient venue. This not only saves borrowers precious time but also mitigates potential transportation expenses, making the mortgage process more accessible and convenient.

Beyond mere procedural efficiency, loan signing agents embody the very essence of industry standards and best practices. They possess an intimate knowledge of the regulations and guidelines governing the mortgage industry, ensuring strict adherence to these norms during the signing process. By upholding these standards, loan signing agents bolster the credibility and trustworthiness of the entire mortgage ecosystem, fostering an environment where borrowers and lenders alike can have confidence in the integrity of their transactions.

Furthermore, loan signing agents serve as guardians against risks and errors that may arise during the mortgage process. They diligently review loan documents for accuracy, completeness, and consistency, leaving no room for ambiguities or omissions that could potentially lead to legal complications. With their meticulous attention to detail and unwavering commitment to best practices, loan signing agents mitigate the risks associated with incorrectly executed or notarized documents, ensuring a smooth and trouble-free mortgage experience for all parties involved.

Loan signing agents are highly valued professionals within the mortgage industry, providing invaluable expertise and services that streamline the signing and notarization of loan documents. Their comprehensive knowledge, meticulous attention to detail, and unwavering commitment to legal compliance make them indispensable figures in the modern mortgage landscape. By engaging the services of a skilled loan signing agent, lenders and borrowers can navigate the complex world of mortgage documentation with confidence, knowing that their transactions are conducted with the utmost professionalism, efficiency, and accuracy.

Understanding the Role of a Loan Signing Agent and Responsibilities Involved

Loan signing agents play a crucial role in the mortgage industry by facilitating loan closings and document signings. The individual's primary duty is to verify that the borrower has accurately completed all the essential paperwork and that it notarizes as per the requirements.

Definition and purpose of a loan signing agent

A loan signing agent assists in the mortgage closing process by facilitating the signing of loan documents between borrowers and lenders. The purpose of this role is to ensure that all required paperwork is correctly signed, notarized, and delivered to the appropriate parties.

Loan signing agents are typically certified notaries public who have undergone additional training specific to the mortgage industry. They must be familiar with various loan documents, including promissory notes, deeds of trust or mortgages, and closing disclosures.

The primary responsibility of a loan signing agent is to guide borrowers through the documentation involved in their mortgage transactions. It includes explaining each document's purpose and ensuring it's appropriately executed according to state laws and regulations.

To perform this job effectively, a loan signing agent must possess excellent communication skills, attention to detail, and knowledge about proper document execution procedures. They should also maintain high levels of accuracy while prioritizing confidentiality throughout every transaction stage.

Working as a loan signing agent can offer opportunities for individuals interested in providing critical services within the real estate industry while enjoying flexible schedules and increased income potential.

Role in facilitating loan closings and document signings

As a loan signing agent, your role in facilitating loan closings and document signings is crucial to the mortgage industry. They have to ensure that all necessary documents are signed by the borrower and properly notarized before being returned to the lender.

One of your primary responsibilities is verifying the identity of each borrower present during a closing appointment. It involves checking their government-issued ID and making sure it matches the name on their loan documents.

You will also review each document with the borrowers to ensure they understand their signing. As an expert in loan documents and signing procedures, you can answer any questions they may have about specific terms or clauses.

During the signing process, you will guide borrowers through each signature line while ensuring all signatures and initials are completed correctly. You must also ensure that any required notarizations are performed accurately according to state-specific guidelines.

Your attention to detail throughout this process ensures that loans close smoothly without errors or delays. Your expertise as a loan signing agent is essential in maintaining trust between lenders, borrowers, and other parties involved in real estate transactions.

Loan signing agents play a crucial role in facilitating loan closings and document signings in the mortgage industry. Their expertise and meticulous attention to detail ensure that the entire process runs smoothly and efficiently, benefiting all parties involved. Let's delve into their specific responsibilities and the value they bring to loan closings and document signings.

1. Document Preparation and Organization:

Loan signing agents take charge of preparing and organizing the necessary loan documents for signing. They ensure that all required forms are complete, accurate, and readily available, saving time and avoiding delays during the closing process. Their expertise in document management allows them to efficiently navigate through the extensive paperwork associated with mortgage transactions.

2. Verification of Identity and Signatures:

One of the essential tasks of a loan signing agent is verifying the identity of the borrowers. They meticulously examine identification documents, compare signatures, and confirm that the individuals present are indeed the authorized signatories. This critical step safeguards against identity theft and fraud, ensuring that the mortgage transaction is conducted with the utmost integrity.

3. Explanation of Documents and Terms:

Loan signing agents play a pivotal role in helping borrowers understand the various loan documents and the terms they contain. They provide clear explanations of complex concepts, allowing borrowers to make informed decisions before signing. By ensuring that borrowers comprehend their obligations, rights, and the financial implications of the loan, loan signing agents empower borrowers to make sound choices that align with their best interests.

4. Compliance with Notarial Requirements:

Notarization is an integral part of the loan closing process, and loan signing agents are well-versed in notarial procedures and requirements. They adhere to strict legal standards, ensuring that all necessary notarial acts are performed accurately and in accordance with applicable laws and regulations. This commitment to compliance reinforces the validity and enforceability of the loan documents.

5. Error-Free Execution of Documents:

Loan signing agents meticulously review loan documents to identify any errors or inconsistencies before the borrowers sign them. Their attention to detail helps identify and rectify potential issues, mitigating the risk of costly mistakes and ensuring that the documents accurately reflect the agreed-upon terms. By facilitating error-free document execution, loan signing agents contribute to the efficiency and smoothness of the loan closing process.

6. Time and Location Flexibility:

Loan signing agents offer borrowers flexibility in terms of time and location for the signing. They understand that borrowers have busy schedules and aim to accommodate their needs by scheduling signings at convenient times and locations. This flexibility helps reduce stress and inconvenience for borrowers, contributing to a positive closing experience.

7. Communication and Coordination:

Loan signing agents act as effective communicators and coordinators throughout the loan closing process. They liaise with various stakeholders, including lenders, title companies, and borrowers, to ensure that all parties are informed and updated on the progress of the signing. Their excellent communication skills and attention to detail minimize misunderstandings and streamline the entire closing process.

8. Professionalism and Trust:

Loan signing agents embody professionalism, instilling confidence and trust in borrowers and other parties involved in the closing. Their expertise, attention to detail, and adherence to legal requirements create an atmosphere of trust and reliability. By conducting themselves in a professional manner, loan signing agents contribute to a positive closing experience, fostering long-term relationships with clients and industry professionals.

Loan signing agents play a vital role in facilitating loan closings and document signings in the mortgage industry. Their responsibilities encompass document preparation, identity verification, explanation of terms, compliance with notarial requirements, error-free execution of documents, and effective communication and coordination. By bringing their expertise, attention to detail, and professionalism to the table, loan signing agents ensure that the loan closing process is efficient, accurate, and conducted with the highest level of integrity.

Familiarity with loan documents and signing procedures

A loan signing agent must become familiar with various loan documents and signing procedures. The fees for a loan may differ based on the which type of loan and the state where it is being signed.

Some standard documents that a loan signing agent may encounter include promissory notes, deeds of trust or mortgages, and disclosure forms. Agents need to understand what each paper entails and its associated legalities.

In addition to understanding individual documents, loan signing agents must know overall signing procedures. It includes knowing how to correctly identify signers, ensuring all necessary signatures are obtained in the correct places, and following any specific instructions provided by lenders or title companies.

This familiarity helps ensure a smooth transaction for all parties involved, increases client satisfaction, and builds trust between the agent and their clients.

Loan signing agents possess an in-depth understanding of loan documents and signing procedures, making them invaluable assets in the mortgage industry. Their expertise allows them to navigate the complexities of loan transactions and ensure that all necessary documents are executed accurately and in accordance with legal requirements. Let's explore the significance of their familiarity with loan documents and signing procedures in greater detail:

1. Comprehensive Knowledge of Loan Documents:

Loan signing agents have a comprehensive understanding of the various loan documents involved in mortgage transactions. They are well-versed in the intricacies of documents such as the promissory note, deed of trust or mortgage, loan estimate, closing disclosure, and other relevant forms. This knowledge enables them to guide borrowers through the signing process, ensuring that all documents are properly reviewed, explained, and executed.

2. Expertise in Document Content and Terms:

Loan signing agents are intimately familiar with the content and terms of loan documents. They possess the ability to decipher complex legal language and financial terminology, allowing them to explain the provisions of the documents to borrowers in a clear and concise manner. By providing comprehensive explanations, loan signing agents help borrowers understand their rights, responsibilities, and obligations, promoting transparency and informed decision-making.

3. Adherence to Signing Procedures:

Loan signing agents are well-versed in the proper procedures for executing loan documents. They understand the specific requirements for each document, such as the number of copies needed, the specific pages that require signatures or initials, and the order in which documents should be signed. This knowledge ensures that all signing procedures are followed accurately, reducing the risk of errors or omissions that could potentially invalidate the documents.

4. Verification of Required Signatures:

Loan signing agents are responsible for verifying that all required signatures are present on the loan documents. They meticulously review each document to ensure that all necessary parties have signed, minimizing the risk of incomplete or invalid documents. This attention to detail ensures that the loan is legally binding and enforceable, providing peace of mind for all parties involved.

5. Compliance with Notary Requirements:

As part of their role, loan signing agents are often commissioned notaries public. This means they have a thorough understanding of the notarial requirements associated with loan documents. They ensure that all notarization procedures are followed accurately, including proper identification of signatories, administration of oaths or affirmations, and completion of notarial certificates. Compliance with notary requirements enhances the validity and enforceability of the loan documents.

6. Keeping Abreast of Regulatory Changes:

Loan signing agents remain updated on the latest regulatory changes that impact loan documents and signing procedures. They stay informed about updates to federal, state, and local laws governing mortgage transactions, ensuring that they operate in full compliance with the evolving legal landscape. This commitment to staying current with regulatory changes guarantees that borrowers receive accurate and up-to-date information during the signing process.

7. Attention to Detail and Accuracy:

Loan signing agents possess a keen eye for detail, meticulously reviewing loan documents for accuracy and completeness. They verify that all required information is included, dates and signatures are properly placed, and any necessary disclosures or addenda are present. By ensuring the accuracy of loan documents, loan signing agents contribute to a smooth and error-free signing process.

In summary, loan signing agents' familiarity with loan documents and signing procedures is paramount to the success and integrity of mortgage transactions. Their comprehensive knowledge of loan documents, expertise in explaining terms, adherence to signing procedures, verification of signatures, compliance with notary requirements, and attention to detail ensure that the signing process is efficient, accurate, and legally sound. Loan signing agents' proficiency in these areas instills confidence in borrowers, lenders, and all parties involved, making them vital contributors to the mortgage industry.

Importance of accuracy, confidentiality, and professionalism

As a loan signing agent, accuracy, confidentiality, and professionalism are essential traits that you must possess. These three elements are crucial to the mortgage industry because errors or discrepancies during loan signings can lead to significant financial losses for all parties involved.

Accuracy is vital when handling loan documents because even a tiny mistake can cause issues. As a loan signing agent, you must ensure that every paper is correctly filled out, signed, and dated by the appropriate parties as required by law. Any mistakes made during this process could result in delays or legal conflicts.

Confidentiality is equally crucial when dealing with sensitive information such as client's personal data and financial records. Loan signing agents can access confidential information that must safeguard. Failure to protect this kind of data can compromise client trust and put careers on the line.

Professionalism also plays an essential role in ensuring successful transactions between lenders and borrowers. Every interaction should be conducted with the utmost respect and courtesy towards clients while maintaining ethical standards of behavior throughout each engagement.

They are accurate, confidential, and professional as a loan signing agent ensures smooth operations in the mortgage industry while always protecting clients' interests.

Accuracy, confidentiality, and professionalism are three key pillars that underpin the success and credibility of loan signing agents in the mortgage industry. These qualities are essential in maintaining the trust of clients and upholding the integrity of the loan signing process. Let's explore the importance of accuracy, confidentiality, and professionalism in greater detail:

1. Accuracy:

The importance of accuracy cannot be overstated in the realm of loan signings. Loan signing agents must exhibit meticulous attention to detail, ensuring that all documents are executed accurately and in accordance with legal requirements. Errors or omissions in loan documents can have significant consequences, potentially leading to legal disputes or financial complications. By prioritizing accuracy, loan signing agents mitigate risks and instill confidence in the parties involved in the transaction.

2. Confidentiality:

Confidentiality is paramount in the mortgage industry, as loan documents contain sensitive and personal information. Loan signing agents are entrusted with handling confidential borrower data, including financial records, social security numbers, and other personal details. Maintaining strict confidentiality safeguards the privacy and trust of borrowers, lenders, and other stakeholders. Loan signing agents must adhere to privacy laws and regulations, implementing secure processes and systems to protect client information. By maintaining confidentiality, loan signing agents contribute to a professional and trustworthy environment.

3. Professionalism:

Professionalism is a cornerstone of the loan signing agent's role. It encompasses a range of attributes, including punctuality, communication skills, and a respectful demeanor. Loan signing agents must present themselves in a professional manner when interacting with clients, maintaining a courteous and business-like demeanor throughout the signing process. Professionalism also extends to being well-prepared, organized, and knowledgeable about loan documents and signing procedures. By embodying professionalism, loan signing agents foster trust and credibility, leaving a positive impression on clients and enhancing the overall borrower experience.

4. Client Satisfaction:

Accuracy, confidentiality, and professionalism directly contribute to client satisfaction. When loan signing agents execute documents accurately, borrowers can trust that the terms and conditions of their loans are correctly represented. By maintaining confidentiality, loan signing agents create a safe environment for borrowers to share their personal information, fostering a sense of security. Additionally, professionalism sets the tone for a smooth and efficient signing process, ensuring that borrowers feel valued and respected. Client satisfaction not only leads to positive word-of-mouth referrals but also strengthens professional relationships and builds a solid reputation in the industry.

5. Legal Compliance:

The commitment to accuracy, confidentiality, and professionalism goes hand in hand with legal compliance. Loan signing agents must adhere to applicable laws, regulations, and industry best practices. They must stay updated on changes in legislation and ensure that their processes align with legal requirements. By upholding legal compliance, loan signing agents protect themselves, clients, and lenders from potential legal consequences or disputes arising from improper handling of loan documents.

In summary, accuracy, confidentiality, and professionalism are essential qualities that loan signing agents must possess to excel in the mortgage industry. By prioritizing accuracy, loan signing agents mitigate risks and instill confidence in the loan signing process. Maintaining strict confidentiality safeguards the privacy of clients, while professionalism enhances client satisfaction and builds trust. Loan signing agents who embody these qualities not only contribute to the success of individual transactions but also foster a positive reputation and long-term relationships with clients and industry partners.

These qualities help build long-lasting relationships with clients based on integrity and trustworthiness — critical components of success for anyone starting their business as a Loan Signing Agent!

Essential Tools and Equipment

As a loan signing agent, you must have all the essential tools and equipment to help facilitate smooth and accurate closings. Having the right tools enables you to perform your job efficiently and enhances your credibility as a professional.

Computer and Internet connection:

As a loan signing agent, having access to a reliable computer and internet connection is crucial. Most of your work will involve communicating with clients, printing and scanning documents, and managing your schedule online.

When choosing a computer for your business, consider one with enough storage space to hold all necessary software programs. It should also have sufficient RAM to ensure smooth operation while running multiple applications simultaneously.

Additionally, ensure you have an internet connection with high-speed data transfer rates. It will help you complete tasks quickly without any interruptions or delays.

Remembering your computer's and internet connection's security is also essential. Install antivirus software on your device and use secure passwords for all accounts.

Proper equipment like computers with fast-speed internet can help streamline client communication and increase productivity.

Printer and scanner:

Access to a printer and scanner is essential to starting your loan signing agent business. In this digital age, most documents send via email or online portals for easy access; however, there will be times when printed paper is required.

The printer and scanner will save you time and money. You'll only go to print shops or rely on others for their printing services. It also allows you to work efficiently from home or any location.

When choosing a printer, consider one that can handle high-volume printing and scanning capabilities, such as duplex (double-sided) scanning, which saves paper usage.

In addition, it's essential to know file formats when handling scanned documents. PDF files are the universal format used in real estate transactions because they preserve formatting and ensure security.

Owning your printer and scanner provides convenience while being cost-effective for your growing business needs.

Mobile Internet Access:

Mobile internet access is essential for loan signing agents who frequently travel to meet clients at various locations. It allows them to access loan documents, communicate with lenders and title companies, and perform necessary research on-the-go. Loan signing agents often rely on mobile hotspot devices or smartphone tethering to ensure a stable internet connection during signings, especially in areas where Wi-Fi access may be limited.

Organization Tools:

Effective organization is crucial for loan signing agents to efficiently manage multiple loan signings and maintain accurate records. They can utilize tools such as file folders, binders, or digital organization software to keep loan documents, borrower information, and other relevant paperwork organized and easily accessible. Implementing a systematic approach to document organization helps prevent errors, ensure compliance, and enhance overall productivity.

Mobile devices and applications:

Mobile devices and applications are essential tools for a loan signing agent business. Using mobile technology, loan signing agents can work remotely and efficiently from anywhere.

One important feature is having access to a reliable smartphone or tablet that allows you to stay connected with clients, receive notifications, and check appointments on the go.

Another crucial aspect is using the proper loan signing software application that fits your needs. These apps can help manage your signings, track appointments, communicate with clients, and even provide digital copies of documents.

Moreover, practical mobile applications like scanning apps let you capture high-quality scans with your phone's camera. It eliminates the need for a traditional scanner while quickly producing clear copies of signed documents.

Utilizing mobile devices and applications in the loan signing agent business helps streamline processes and increase productivity by providing accessibility anywhere.

Required software and notary tools

You should have the right tools and software. You will also want to invest in reliable internet service and a laptop or tablet to access your documents easily.

In addition, it is essential to have notary tools such as stamps, embossing seals, and journals. These items are necessary for verifying signatures on legal documents and maintaining accurate records.

Notary-specific software programs like Notarize.com offer electronic signature capabilities, document storage options, and appointment scheduling features.

Other helpful software includes cloud-based file-sharing services like Dropbox or Google Drive, which allow you to securely share files with clients while keeping them organized in one place.

Investing in the necessary hardware and software tools for your loan signing business ensures that you provide efficient and professional services to your clients.

Loan signing agents rely on specific software and notary tools to efficiently perform their duties in the mortgage industry. These tools help streamline document management, facilitate secure electronic signatures, and ensure compliance with notarial requirements. Let's explore some of the essential software and notary tools that loan signing agents need:

1. Electronic Document Management Systems:

Loan signing agents utilize electronic document management systems to store, organize, and access loan documents securely. These systems allow agents to upload, manage, and share documents with clients, lenders, and title companies. Electronic document management systems also enable loan signing agents to track document versions, ensure accuracy, and maintain an organized record of loan signings.

2. Electronic Signature Platforms:

With the increasing prevalence of digital transactions, loan signing agents often rely on electronic signature platforms to facilitate remote signing processes. These platforms enable borrowers to sign loan documents electronically, eliminating the need for physical signatures and mailing documents. Loan signing agents use electronic signature platforms to guide borrowers through the signing process, ensuring all necessary documents are signed, initialed, and dated accurately.

3. Notary Journal Software:

Maintaining a notary journal is a critical component of a loan signing agent's responsibilities. Notary journal software provides a digital solution for recording and managing notarial acts. These tools enable loan signing agents to capture essential details, such as the date and time of the notarization, the type of document, the signatories, and any relevant identification details. Notary journal software helps ensure compliance with notarial recordkeeping requirements.

4. Notary Stamps and Seals:

As commissioned notaries public, loan signing agents must possess a notary stamp and seal. These physical tools are used to imprint an official notary seal on loan documents, providing authentication of the notarial act. Loan signing agents should ensure their notary stamps and seals meet state-specific requirements and include the necessary information, such as their name, commission expiration date, and commissioning state.

5. Encryption and Security Tools:

Loan signing agents handle sensitive borrower information, and it is crucial to protect this data from unauthorized access. Encryption and security tools help safeguard electronic documents, ensuring that personal and financial information remains confidential. Loan signing agents should utilize secure file transfer protocols, password protection, and encryption technologies to enhance the security of loan documents and maintain compliance with data privacy regulations.

6. Mobile Notary Tools:

Mobile notary tools, such as portable scanners and printers, enable loan signing agents to perform notarizations on the go. These tools are particularly useful when meeting clients outside of an office setting. Portable scanners allow loan signing agents to capture high-quality digital copies of documents, while portable printers enable them to produce printed copies for clients during the signing process. Mobile notary tools enhance the convenience and flexibility of loan signings.

7. Remote Communication and Collaboration Tools:

Loan signing agents often need to communicate and collaborate with clients, lenders, and title companies remotely. Remote communication tools, such as video conferencing platforms, email, and secure messaging applications, facilitate seamless communication and real-time collaboration. These tools allow loan signing agents to discuss signing details, address questions or concerns, and exchange necessary documents efficiently, regardless of physical distance.

Loan signing agents rely on specific software and notary tools to optimize their workflow and ensure compliance with industry standards. Electronic document management systems, electronic signature platforms, notary journal software, notary stamps and seals, encryption and security tools, mobile notary tools, and remote communication and collaboration tools are essential for loan signing agents to carry out their responsibilities effectively. By leveraging these tools, loan signing agents can enhance efficiency, maintain accuracy, and provide a seamless experience for clients in the mortgage industry.

Building a Professional Network and Finding Clients

It is the most critical aspect of starting a loan signing agent business. It means connecting with potential clients and other professionals in the real estate industry will boost your work, such as escrow officers, title companies, real estate agents, and mortgage brokers.

In the highly competitive world of the loan signing agent business, building a strong professional network and attracting clients are essential ingredients for success. Loan signing agents must proactively establish connections within the industry and employ effective strategies to attract a steady stream of clients. Let's delve into the significance of building a professional network and explore effective methods for client acquisition.

One of the fundamental strategies in building a professional network is to engage actively within the industry. Attending industry events, such as conferences, seminars, and workshops, offers valuable opportunities to meet fellow professionals and establish meaningful connections. Engaging in conversations, exchanging contact information, and following up afterward are crucial steps in nurturing these connections and fostering mutually beneficial relationships.

Joining professional associations and organizations dedicated to notaries and loan signing agents can also significantly contribute to expanding one's network. These associations provide networking events, educational resources, and online forums where professionals can connect, exchange ideas, and share insights. Actively participating in these communities helps loan signing agents establish themselves as reputable experts in the field and gain visibility among potential clients.

Collaborating with industry partners, such as lenders, title companies, and real estate professionals, can also play a pivotal role in expanding one's network and attracting clients. By forging mutually beneficial relationships, loan signing agents can position themselves as reliable and trustworthy partners. Offering educational sessions or workshops on loan signing procedures and industry trends can be an effective way to provide value to these partners, leading to increased referrals and a broader client base.

In the digital age, an online presence is paramount for loan signing agents. Creating a professional website or leveraging social media platforms can help showcase expertise, demonstrate professionalism, and attract potential clients. Sharing valuable content, such as informative articles, tips, and insights related to loan signings and the mortgage industry, establishes credibility and positions loan signing agents as trusted authorities in their field.

Another effective approach to building a professional network and attracting clients is through client referrals. Providing exceptional service and exceeding client expectations not only leads to satisfied clients but also increases the likelihood of them recommending the loan signing agent to others. Building strong relationships with clients, maintaining open lines of communication, and consistently delivering outstanding service are essential in generating positive word-of-mouth and expanding the client base.

Building a professional network and finding clients are integral aspects of success for loan signing agents. Actively engaging within the industry, attending events, joining professional associations, collaborating with industry partners, establishing an online presence, and fostering client relationships are key strategies in this pursuit. By nurturing a strong professional network and employing effective client acquisition methods, loan signing agents can enhance their visibility, attract clients, and position themselves as trusted professionals in the mortgage industry.

Identifying and Marketing to Potential Clients

Identifying and marketing to potential clients is crucial to establishing a successful loan signing agent business. You must identify key individuals and organizations within the real estate and mortgage industry to reach your target audience effectively. Start by targeting real estate agents, brokers, and loan officers who frequently work with homebuyers.

These professionals can refer their clients to you for loan signing services. Additionally, reach out to attorneys and title companies involved in real estate transactions, as they often require the assistance of loan signing agents.

Networking with local business associations and attending industry events can increase connections with potential clients. Develop a compelling marketing strategy highlighting your expertise, professionalism, and ability to streamline the loan signing process. Utilize online platforms, such as a professional website and social media, to showcase your services and engage with your target market. By effectively identifying and marketing to potential clients, you can establish valuable partnerships and generate a steady stream of business for your loan signing agent business.

In the competitive landscape of the loan signing agent business, identifying and effectively marketing to potential clients is crucial for sustained success. Loan signing agents need to implement strategies that allow them to identify their target audience and engage with them in a way that showcases their expertise and value. Let's explore the process of identifying and marketing to potential clients, highlighting key considerations and effective methods.

The first step in this process is understanding your target audience. Loan signing agents should conduct market research to identify the key players in the mortgage industry who require their services. This includes lenders, title companies, real estate agents, and mortgage brokers. By identifying the specific needs and pain points of these potential clients, loan signing agents can tailor their marketing efforts to address these concerns effectively.

Once the target audience has been identified, loan signing agents can develop a comprehensive marketing strategy. This strategy should include both online and offline tactics to maximize reach and engagement. Building an online presence through a professional website, blog, or social media platforms allows loan signing agents to showcase their expertise and provide valuable content that resonates with their target audience. Consistently creating and sharing informative articles, tips, and insights related to loan signings and the mortgage industry helps establish credibility and positions loan signing agents as trusted authorities.

In addition to an online presence, loan signing agents should also engage in offline marketing efforts. This can include attending industry events, such as conferences or trade shows, where they can network with potential clients face-to-face. Distributing business cards, brochures, or other promotional materials at these events can leave a lasting impression and serve as a reminder of the loan signing agent's services.

Networking is a powerful tool in identifying and marketing to potential clients. Building relationships with industry professionals, such as lenders, title companies, and real estate agents, can lead to valuable referrals and collaborations. Engaging in meaningful conversations, attending industry networking events, and offering to provide educational sessions or workshops can help loan signing agents establish themselves as trusted partners within the mortgage industry.

Word-of-mouth marketing is another effective strategy for attracting potential clients. Providing exceptional service, exceeding client expectations, and maintaining open lines of communication with existing clients can generate positive recommendations and referrals. Loan signing agents should focus on building strong relationships with their clients, ensuring their needs are met, and consistently delivering outstanding service.

Monitoring and adapting marketing efforts is crucial for success. Loan signing agents should track the effectiveness of their marketing strategies, measuring key performance indicators and adjusting their approach as needed. By analyzing the data and feedback received, loan signing agents can refine their marketing efforts, ensuring they resonate with potential clients and generate the desired results.

Identifying and marketing to potential clients requires a targeted approach that addresses the needs and concerns of the mortgage industry. By conducting market research, developing a comprehensive marketing strategy, building an online presence, engaging in offline marketing efforts, networking with industry professionals, and focusing on exceptional service, loan signing agents can attract and retain a steady stream of potential clients. Through continuous monitoring and adaptation, loan signing agents can refine their marketing efforts and position themselves as trusted professionals in the field.

Understanding Your Local Market

Understanding your local market is one of the most critical factors in starting a successful loan signing agent business. It means researching the demand for notary services and identifying potential clients and competitors in your area.

To begin, research the real estate industry in your region by looking at housing trends and analyzing mortgage rates. You will better understand how busy the market may be and anticipate when you might see an influx of business.

Additionally, identify other signing agents or mobile notaries operating within your area. Analyze their marketing strategies and pricing models to determine what differentiates you.

Another helpful strategy is establishing relationships with local lenders, brokers, escrow companies, title companies, and real estate agents. They can provide valuable insights into the needs of borrowers in your community while also providing referrals that could lead to new business opportunities.

Ultimately, a thorough understanding of your local market will enable you to tailor marketing campaigns accordingly while anticipating trends before they occur.

In the world of loan signing agents, having a comprehensive understanding of your local market is key to achieving success. Each market has its own intricacies, dynamics, and regulations that significantly influence how loan signing agents operate. By gaining in-depth knowledge of your local market, you can tailor your services, marketing strategies, and client interactions to effectively meet the unique needs of your target audience. Let's explore the significance of understanding your local market and how it can shape your business decisions.

To begin, conducting thorough market research is essential. This involves delving into the local demographics, real estate landscape, lending practices, and economic climate. By analyzing this wealth of information, you can identify prevailing trends, preferences, and opportunities specific to your local market.

Equally important is familiarizing yourself with local regulations and requirements. Different jurisdictions may have specific rules and guidelines that loan signing agents must adhere to. Staying informed and compliant with these regulations is crucial to ensuring that your business operates legally and ethically within your local market.

Establishing strong relationships with local industry professionals is another vital aspect of understanding your local market. Real estate agents, lenders, title companies, and other key players in the mortgage industry can offer invaluable insights into local practices, client preferences, and industry trends. By forging connections and engaging in meaningful conversations with these professionals, you can gain a deeper understanding of the dynamics at play in your local market.

It's equally important to keep a watchful eye on the competition within your local market. Analyzing the services, pricing, and reputation of other loan signing agents operating in the area can provide valuable insights. This knowledge can help you position yourself strategically by identifying gaps in the market or by highlighting your unique value propositions to attract clients who are seeking specialized expertise or a fresh approach.

Engaging with the local community is yet another effective way to grasp the nuances of your local market. Participating in local events, joining community organizations, and supporting local causes not only helps you establish a positive reputation but also provides firsthand insights into the needs and preferences of the local community.

Regularly evaluating and adjusting your business strategies based on the insights gained from understanding your local market is essential for long-term success. By staying abreast of market trends, actively seeking feedback from clients and industry professionals, and adapting your practices accordingly, you can remain competitive and relevant in your local market.

Gaining a deep understanding of your local market empowers loan signing agents to tailor their services, marketing strategies, and client interactions effectively. Through thorough market research, compliance with local regulations, building relationships with industry professionals, analyzing competition, engaging with the local community, and continually adapting business strategies, loan signing agents can position themselves as trusted professionals who meet the unique needs of their local market.

Building Relationships with Local Escrow and Title Companies

Establish solid relationships with local escrow and title companies to build a successful loan signing agent business. These businesses are integral players in the real estate industry, providing critical support to those buying or selling property.

To begin building these relationships, start by introducing yourself to representatives from these companies. Attend events where they may be present, such as real estate networking meetings or trade shows. You should use business cards and marketing materials so they can familiarize themselves with your services.

Once you have made initial contact, following up is essential. Stay top-of-mind by sending periodic emails or newsletters highlighting any recent achievements or new skills you've added to your repertoire.

Another way to build strong relationships with escrow and title companies is by providing excellent service on every assignment. Ensure all documents are correctly filled out and submitted promptly – this will impress clients and increase their likelihood of referring others needing similar services.

Remember that professional relationships take time to develop. It's essential to keep going even if things don't happen overnight - persistence pays off! Keep reaching out and nurturing those connections until trust is established between both parties.

Establishing strong relationships with local escrow and title companies is a crucial aspect of success for loan signing agents. These companies play a vital role in the mortgage industry, handling the closing process and ensuring the legality and transfer of property titles. By fostering meaningful connections with escrow and title companies in your local market, you can position yourself as a trusted partner and increase your chances of receiving consistent referrals. Let's delve into the importance of building relationships with local escrow and title companies and explore effective strategies for establishing and nurturing these connections.

First and foremost, it's essential to understand the role that escrow and title companies play in the mortgage industry. Escrow companies act as neutral third parties, holding and disbursing funds during the closing process, while title companies ensure that the property's title is clear and can be legally transferred. Recognizing their significance and demonstrating your knowledge of their functions will help you build credibility and establish a solid foundation for building relationships.

A proactive approach is crucial when reaching out to local escrow and title companies. Introduce yourself as a professional loan signing agent and express your interest in collaborating with them. Take the time to research and identify the key escrow and title companies in your local market, and then make personalized connections. Attend industry events, such as conferences or networking gatherings, where you can interact face-to-face and begin establishing rapport.

When engaging with escrow and title company representatives, it's essential to communicate your expertise and commitment to professionalism. Highlight your understanding of the loan signing process, including the importance of accuracy, attention to detail, and adherence to legal requirements. Emphasize the value you bring to the table as a reliable and efficient partner in facilitating smooth and error-free loan closings.

Offering educational sessions or workshops to escrow and title company staff can be an effective way to demonstrate your knowledge and expertise. By providing insights into loan signing procedures, common challenges, and emerging trends in the industry, you position yourself as a valuable resource. This not only helps strengthen your relationships with these companies but also increases the likelihood of receiving referrals and gaining a competitive edge in the market.

Maintaining open lines of communication is vital for nurturing these relationships. Regularly follow up with the contacts you have made at escrow and title companies, providing updates on industry developments, sharing relevant resources, and offering assistance whenever needed. By staying top-of-mind and demonstrating your commitment to their success, you enhance the likelihood of receiving referrals and building a lasting partnership.

It's important to remember that building relationships with local escrow and title companies is a long-term endeavor. Cultivating trust and rapport takes time and consistent effort. Actively seek feedback from your contacts within these companies, asking for suggestions on how you can improve your services or better meet their needs. Incorporating their input into your practices demonstrates your dedication to continuous improvement and strengthens the bond between you and these industry partners.

Building relationships with local escrow and title companies is a critical step for loan signing agents looking to expand their business. By understanding the functions of these companies, taking a proactive approach, demonstrating expertise and professionalism, offering educational sessions, maintaining open lines of communication, and incorporating feedback into your practices, you can establish strong partnerships that lead to a steady flow of referrals and long-term success.

Marketing Yourself to Lenders and Mortgage Brokers

Once you've established your business as a loan signing agent and built a professional network, it's time to start marketing yourself to lenders and mortgage brokers. You should prepare a list of potential clients in your area. You take this information online or by contacting local real estate associations.

Next, create marketing materials that highlight your qualifications and experience. It can include a website, social media profiles, brochures, and business cards. Make sure these materials are polished and professional-looking.

To interact at industry events or conferences where you can meet potential clients face-to-face. Ensure you have a concise pitch to explain your services and how they differ from other loan signing agents.

Another effective way to market yourself is through referrals from satisfied clients. Encourage current clients to refer their friends or colleagues who may need loan signing services.

Remember that building relationships with lenders and mortgage brokers takes time and effort. Continue to follow up with potential clients regularly without being pushy or aggressive.

Starting a loan signing agent business requires dedication, hard work, and patience. It would help to have the necessary equipment like a computer, internet connection, printer and scanner, and mobile devices with the required applications.

Building relationships with local escrow and title companies is crucial for finding clients, as they can provide you with regular assignments. Understanding your local market helps you identify potential customers requiring your services.

Marketing yourself to lenders and mortgage brokers expands your reach beyond escrow and title companies. A professional network will also help in building your reputation in the industry.

It's essential to keep up-to-date with new loan signing regulations or laws affecting your business.

Effectively marketing yourself to lenders and mortgage brokers is crucial for loan signing agents who want to establish strong relationships and secure a consistent stream of business. These professionals play a key role in the mortgage industry, connecting borrowers with loan products and facilitating the loan process. By showcasing your skills, professionalism, and value proposition, you can position yourself as a trusted and reliable partner for lenders and mortgage brokers. Let's explore some effective strategies for marketing yourself to this important audience.

First and foremost, it's essential to understand the needs and preferences of lenders and mortgage brokers. Put yourself in their shoes and consider what they value in a loan signing agent. Timeliness, accuracy, attention to detail, and strong communication skills are traits that lenders and brokers often prioritize. Tailor your marketing messages to highlight these qualities and demonstrate how you can meet their expectations.

Building a strong online presence is paramount in today's digital age. Create a professional website that showcases your expertise, services, and testimonials from satisfied clients. Ensure that your website is user-friendly and optimized for search engines so that lenders and mortgage brokers can easily find you when searching for loan signing agents in their area.

Utilize social media platforms strategically to promote your services and engage with your target audience. Share educational content, industry updates, and success stories to position yourself as an authority in the field. Actively participate in online communities, such as industry forums or LinkedIn groups, where lenders and mortgage brokers gather. By providing valuable insights and engaging in meaningful conversations, you can build credibility and expand your network.

Networking is a powerful tool for marketing yourself to lenders and mortgage brokers. Attend industry conferences, seminars, and trade shows where you can connect with these professionals face-to-face. Be prepared with professional business cards and a compelling elevator pitch that clearly communicates your unique value proposition. Engage in conversations, ask questions, and listen attentively to understand their specific needs. Follow up with personalized messages or handwritten notes to reinforce the connection and express your interest in collaborating.

Referrals can be a valuable source of business from lenders and mortgage brokers. Proactively seek referrals by establishing and nurturing relationships with professionals in related industries, such as real estate agents, appraisers, or home inspectors. Offer to provide educational sessions or workshops to their teams to showcase your expertise and build trust. When you consistently deliver exceptional service, lenders and mortgage brokers will be more likely to refer you to their clients and colleagues.

Consider developing strategic partnerships with select lenders or mortgage brokers. Collaborating on joint marketing efforts, such as hosting educational webinars or creating informative content together, can benefit both parties and help expand your reach. By aligning yourself with reputable professionals in the industry, you enhance your credibility and increase your chances of being recommended to borrowers.

Lastly, always strive for excellence in your work. Consistently provide exceptional service, pay attention to details, and communicate promptly and professionally. Positive word-of-mouth referrals from satisfied lenders and mortgage brokers can be a powerful marketing tool that can significantly impact your business.

In conclusion, marketing yourself effectively to lenders and mortgage brokers requires a strategic approach. Understand their needs and preferences, build a strong online presence, utilize social media and networking opportunities, seek referrals, develop strategic partnerships, and consistently deliver exceptional service. By implementing these strategies, you can position yourself as a trusted and reliable loan signing agent, gaining the attention and business of lenders and mortgage brokers in your market.

Chapter 4

Business Setup and Administration

Beginning a notary business can be an exhilarating and fulfilling experience but involves significant administrative duties. From choosing the proper business structure to obtaining necessary licenses and permits, there are several steps you need to take before officially opening your doors for business. In this chapter, we'll guide you through setting up and administrating a successful notary business that complies with all legal requirements.

Choosing a business structure (sole proprietorship, partnership, LLC, etc.)

When starting a notary public and loan signing agent business, one important decision you need to make is choosing the right business structure. The business structure you select will have implications for various aspects of your operation, including legal responsibilities, taxation, liability protection, and management flexibility. It's crucial to carefully consider the options available to you and select the structure that best aligns with your goals and circumstances. Let's explore the different business structures commonly used by notary public and loan signing agents, including sole proprietorship, partnership, limited liability company (LLC), and more.

Sole Proprietorship:

A sole proprietorship is the simplest form of business structure and is often chosen by individuals starting a small-scale operation on their own. As a sole proprietor, you have complete control over your business and its decision-making processes. You are personally responsible for all aspects of your business, including liabilities and debts. From a tax perspective, the income and expenses of the business are reported on your personal tax return.

Partnership:

If you plan to start your business with one or more partners, a partnership structure may be suitable. There are two main types of partnerships: general partnerships and limited partnerships. In a general partnership, all partners share equal responsibilities and liabilities. In a limited partnership, there is at least one general partner who assumes unlimited liability, while the limited partners have limited liability but limited control over the business. Partnerships require a partnership agreement that outlines the roles, responsibilities, and profit-sharing arrangements among the partners.

Limited Liability Company (LLC):

Many notary public and loan signing agents opt for forming a limited liability company (LLC) due to the benefits it offers. An LLC provides a level of personal liability protection for its owners, known as members. This means that members' personal assets are typically protected from business liabilities. LLCs also offer flexibility in terms of management structure, allowing members to choose between member-managed and manager-managed structures. From a tax perspective, an LLC can be treated as a disregarded entity (similar to a sole proprietorship) or elect to be taxed as a partnership or even a corporation.

Corporation:

Forming a corporation is a more complex process but offers certain advantages, particularly when it comes to liability protection and raising capital. Corporations are separate legal entities from their owners, known as shareholders. Shareholders have limited liability, meaning their personal assets are generally shielded from business debts and liabilities. Corporations have a more formal structure, with officers, directors, and bylaws governing their operations. From a tax standpoint, corporations are subject to corporate income tax, and shareholders may also be subject to taxes on dividends and capital gains.

Professional Corporation (PC):

For notary public and loan signing agents who are licensed professionals, such as attorneys or accountants, forming a professional corporation (PC) may be a suitable option. A PC is a specific type of corporation that provides liability protection for professional services rendered by its shareholders. The formation and operation of a PC typically involve compliance with specific regulations and licensing requirements applicable to the profession.

Each business structure has its own advantages and considerations, and the right choice for your notary public and loan signing agent business will depend on factors such as your personal circumstances, long-term goals, risk tolerance, and tax implications. Consulting with a qualified attorney or tax professional can provide valuable guidance in making this decision.

When choosing a business structure, it's important to consider the legal and financial implications it may have on your business. Factors such as liability protection, taxation, management structure, ease of formation, and ongoing compliance requirements should all be carefully evaluated. Additionally, keep in mind that your chosen structure is not set in stone and can be modified as your business grows or evolves.

Selecting the appropriate business structure is a critical step when establishing a notary public and loan signing agent business. Carefully weigh the advantages and considerations associated with each structure, including sole proprietorship, partnership, LLC, corporation, or professional corporation, to determine which best aligns with your specific needs and goals. Remember to seek professional advice to ensure that you make an informed decision that sets a solid foundation for your business's success.

Registering the business structure with the appropriate authorities

The primary step in setting up a notary business is registering your chosen business structure with the relevant authorities. This step will allow your business to be recognized as a legal entity and operate without legal issues.

The process starts with choosing a suitable business, like a sole proprietorship, partnership, or LLC. Every structure has pros and cons, so it's crucial to research before deciding.

Once you've decided on your preferred structure, register with the relevant authorities in the next step. It depends on your choice; you may need to submit documents such as Articles of Incorporation or Articles of Organization.

It's essential to ensure you're filing all necessary paperwork correctly and paying any associated fees accurately. Any missteps during this process could result in unnecessary delays or complications down the road.

In addition to registering your business structure, you must obtain any required permits or certifications to operate a notary service. These details can differ from state to state, including background checks or fingerprinting before permission to offer notarial services within that jurisdiction.

Registering your chosen business structure is integral to a successful notary service. It ensures both legality and credibility while allowing you to focus on delivering top-notch services confidently.

Registering the chosen business name with the appropriate authorities

Registering your business name selected is critical when setting up a notary business. It ensures you have all the rights to use the name for your business and helps prevent any confusion with other companies.

Before registering your business name, it's essential to do thorough research to ensure that another company still needs to start using it. You can check this by searching online databases or contacting the appropriate authorities.

Once you've confirmed that your desired business name is available, you'll need to register it with the relevant authorities in your state.

It usually means filing paperwork with the Secretary of State's office or local county clerk.

All details are required during the registration process. Ensure all necessary documents are on hand before beginning the registration process.

After successfully registering your business name, it's essential to ensure that all promotional materials, such as websites, social media accounts, and advertising, reflect this new branding.

Registering a unique and memorable brand name is crucial for establishing credibility in the marketplace while avoiding legal disputes over intellectual property rights down the road.

Researching the specific licensing requirements for a notary business

Before diving into the world of notary public and loan signing agent business, it's essential to understand and comply with the specific licensing requirements in your jurisdiction. Licensing regulations ensure that notaries operate within legal boundaries, maintain the integrity of their services, and protect the public's interests. In this section, we will explore the importance of researching and understanding the licensing requirements for a notary business, as well as provide insights into the general process and considerations involved.

Licensing requirements for notary businesses can vary from one jurisdiction to another, whether it's a state, province, or country. Therefore, it is crucial to conduct thorough research to identify the specific regulations and prerequisites that apply to your location. Start by reviewing the laws, statutes, and regulations governing notaries in your jurisdiction. This information is typically available on the website of the appropriate government agency responsible for overseeing notary services. Take the time to familiarize yourself with the legal framework, as it will serve as your guide throughout the licensing process.

In addition to legal requirements, it's important to understand the qualifications and prerequisites for becoming a notary public. Typically, these include age restrictions, residency requirements, and educational prerequisites. Some jurisdictions may require completion of a notary training course or passing an examination to demonstrate your knowledge and understanding of notarial practices and procedures. Familiarize yourself with these qualifications to ensure you meet the necessary criteria before proceeding further.

Once you have a clear understanding of the legal and educational requirements, the next step is to gather the necessary documentation to support your application. This may include personal identification documents, proof of residency, educational certificates, and any other supporting materials specified by the licensing authority. Keep in mind that certain jurisdictions may also require applicants to obtain a surety bond or errors and omissions insurance to provide additional protection for clients.

As you navigate through the licensing process, it's important to stay organized and maintain accurate records. Keep a detailed record of all the steps you have taken, including the documents you have gathered, any training or exams you have completed, and any fees paid. This documentation will serve as proof of your compliance and can be beneficial in case of any future inquiries or audits.

In some jurisdictions, notary applicants may be required to undergo a background check or provide character references. This is done to ensure that notaries possess the moral character and trustworthiness necessary to perform their duties. Be prepared to provide the necessary information and cooperate fully with any background checks or reference requests.

It's worth noting that licensing requirements may change over time due to legislative updates or regulatory changes. Therefore, it's essential to stay informed and regularly check for any updates or amendments to the licensing requirements in your jurisdiction. Subscribing to newsletters, joining professional associations, or establishing connections with other notaries in your area can help you stay abreast of any changes and industry updates.

In addition to the specific licensing requirements, it's important to develop a comprehensive understanding of the code of ethics and professional conduct expected of notaries. Familiarize yourself with the principles of integrity, impartiality, confidentiality, and accuracy that underpin the notarial profession. Embracing these ethical standards will not only enhance your professional reputation but also contribute to the overall integrity of the notary public and loan signing agent industry.

Lastly, it's crucial to approach the licensing process with patience and persistence. Obtaining a notary license requires time, effort, and dedication. Be prepared to navigate through any potential challenges or delays that may arise during the application process. Remember that compliance with licensing requirements is essential for operating a legitimate and reputable notary business, and it serves as a foundation for building trust with clients and industry professionals.

Conducting thorough research and understanding the specific licensing requirements for a notary business is paramount. By familiarizing yourself with the legal framework, educational prerequisites, documentation requirements, and ethical standards, you will position yourself for success in the notary public and loan signing agent industry. Stay informed, organized, and diligent throughout the licensing process, and embrace the responsibilities and obligations that come with being a licensed notary. Your commitment to compliance will contribute to the professionalism and integrity of the industry as a whole.

Applying for a business license from the relevant licensing agency

After finalizing the business structure and registering the chosen name, the next step in setting up a notary business is to apply for a business license. Depending on your location, this license is issued by the relevant licensing agency in your state or country.

First, research the best agency which handles business licenses for notaries in your area. The licensing requirements may differ based on location and type of notary service provided. Be sure to review all application guidelines thoroughly before applying.

Most agencies offer online applications; however, some require physical forms submitted via mail or in-person visits. Ensure that all the necessary documentation, including identification cards and certificate copies, if applicable, are included with your application.

Some states may require background checks or fingerprinting before issuing a license. These steps can add time and expense to the process; therefore, it's advisable to plan accordingly.

Once you have submitted your application and any additional documents requested by authorities (such as proof of liability insurance), allow ample time for processing before following up with relevant parties about its status.

Applying for a business license can be cumbersome, but completing this step ensures that you comply with law regulations while assuring customers that they work closely with reputable professionals who follow legal protocols.

Obtaining any necessary permits or certifications for operating a notary business

In summary, setting up and administering a business requires careful consideration of various legal requirements. Business owners must choose the proper business structure, register it with the appropriate authorities, and obtain all necessary permits and certifications to operate in their state.

While there may be some challenges, taking these steps will ensure that your notary business is set up for success. Stay organized throughout the process and seek guidance from reputable sources such as legal experts or industry associations.

By following these guidelines, you can confidently establish your notary business while complying with all relevant laws and regulations. Dedication and hard work can make your notary services invaluable to your community.

Establishing and operating a successful notary business requires more than just obtaining the necessary licensing. In addition to meeting the legal requirements, you may also need to acquire specific permits and certifications to ensure compliance with local regulations and industry standards. These additional authorizations demonstrate your commitment to professionalism and provide added assurance to clients. Let's explore the importance of securing such permits and certifications and delve into the process involved.

To begin, it is crucial to conduct thorough research to identify any permits or certifications required by your jurisdiction or industry. Start by reaching out to the appropriate government agencies responsible for overseeing notary services in your area. These agencies can provide you with valuable information regarding any additional authorizations needed to operate legally as a notary public and loan signing agent.

One common permit that you may need to acquire is a business license or permit. This permit grants you official permission to conduct business within your local jurisdiction while ensuring compliance with local laws and regulations. The specific requirements and application process for a business license can vary depending on your location. It is imperative to research and follow the guidelines provided by the relevant authority to obtain this essential permit.

In addition to a business license, you may also consider pursuing specialized certifications or professional designations to further enhance your credentials and expertise. These certifications demonstrate your commitment to continuous professional development and can provide you with a competitive edge in the industry. Examples of certifications commonly sought by notary public and loan signing agents include the Certified Notary Signing Agent (CNSA) and Certified Loan Signing Agent (CLSA) designations. To earn these certifications, you will likely need to complete specific training programs and pass rigorous examinations that validate your knowledge and proficiency in notarial practices and loan document signings.

It is important to note that industry-specific permits or certifications may also be required, depending on the nature of your notary business. For example, if you plan to offer remote online notarization services, you may need to obtain a separate authorization or certification to perform these digital transactions legally. Remote online notarization has gained popularity due to technological advancements and the demand for convenient and secure document signings. Familiarize yourself with the regulations and requirements specific to remote online notarization in your jurisdiction to ensure compliance with the law.

Furthermore, if your notary business aims to provide specialized services or cater to specific industries, additional permits or certifications may be necessary. These requirements vary depending on the jurisdiction and the nature of the services provided. Consulting with legal professionals or industry associations can provide valuable guidance on the specific permits or certifications required for your particular business activities.

The process of obtaining permits and certifications for your notary business typically involves submitting applications, providing relevant documentation, and potentially undergoing inspections or assessments. It is crucial to carefully follow the instructions provided by the issuing authorities, ensuring that all required forms and supporting materials are complete and accurate. Be prepared to fulfill any associated fees and adhere to ongoing compliance requirements, such as permit renewals or completing continuing education courses.

Maintaining compliance with the necessary permits and certifications is vital for operating a legitimate and reputable notary business. Failure to obtain and maintain these authorizations can lead to legal consequences and tarnish your professional reputation. Regularly review and update your permits and certifications as required by law and industry standards, staying informed of any changes or updates that may impact your business operations.

Securing the necessary permits and certifications for your notary business is a critical step in demonstrating your commitment to professionalism, enhancing your credibility, and ensuring compliance with local regulations and industry standards. By conducting thorough research, diligently following the application process, and fulfilling ongoing compliance requirements, you will establish a solid foundation for operating a successful notary business.

Accounting and Financial Management

Accounting and financial management are vital to any successful business. Proper bookkeeping is essential for keeping track of income, expenses, and taxes.

In the world of business, effective accounting and financial management are essential components of success. As a notary public and loan signing agent, understanding and implementing sound financial practices are critical for running a profitable and sustainable business. This section will delve into the importance of accounting and financial management for notary businesses and provide insights on how to establish and maintain solid financial systems.

Accurate accounting and financial management play a vital role in the day-to-day operations of a notary business. It involves recording, organizing, and analyzing financial transactions, as well as developing strategies to optimize revenue, manage expenses, and ensure compliance with tax regulations. By maintaining comprehensive and transparent financial records, you gain valuable insights into the financial health of your business and make informed decisions that drive growth.

One of the first steps in establishing effective financial management is to separate your personal and business finances. Opening a dedicated business bank account allows you to track and manage your business transactions separately from your personal expenses. This separation simplifies record-keeping, facilitates tax reporting, and provides a clear picture of your business's financial performance.

Implementing a robust bookkeeping system is crucial for tracking income, expenses, and financial transactions. Consider using accounting software or hiring a professional bookkeeper to maintain accurate and up-to-date financial records. This software can streamline tasks such as invoicing, expense tracking, and generating financial reports, saving you time and reducing the risk of errors.

Regularly reconciling your bank statements with your financial records is essential to identify any discrepancies or errors. This process helps ensure the accuracy of your financial information and provides a clear overview of your cash flow. Reconciliation involves comparing your bank statement transactions with your recorded transactions, adjusting for any outstanding checks, deposits, or fees, and resolving any discrepancies.

Maintaining a budget is another crucial aspect of financial management. A budget allows you to plan and allocate funds effectively, control expenses, and identify areas for potential cost savings. Start by analyzing your revenue streams and fixed expenses, such as office rent, utilities, and insurance. Then, allocate funds for variable expenses, such as marketing, professional development, and equipment maintenance. Regularly review and adjust your budget to reflect changing circumstances and financial goals.

Monitoring your cash flow is paramount to the financial health of your notary business. Cash flow refers to the inflow and outflow of money within your business over a specific period. A positive cash flow ensures that you have sufficient funds to cover expenses, invest in growth opportunities, and manage unforeseen expenses. Regularly analyze your cash flow statement to identify trends, plan for cash reserves, and address any potential cash flow issues proactively.

Proper tax planning and compliance are critical for notary businesses. Stay informed about local, state, and federal tax regulations that apply to your business. Consider consulting with a tax professional or accountant to ensure that you are meeting your tax obligations, taking advantage of any available deductions or credits, and minimizing your tax liability. Accurate and timely tax filings help avoid penalties and maintain your business's financial integrity.

Another aspect of financial management to consider is managing your business's accounts receivable and accounts payable. Promptly invoicing clients and following up on unpaid invoices ensures a steady cash flow. Implement a systematic approach to tracking and collecting payments, including establishing clear payment terms, sending timely reminders, and employing effective collection strategies when necessary. On the other hand, managing your accounts payable involves paying vendors and suppliers on time to maintain positive relationships and prevent any disruptions in your operations.

Regular financial analysis is crucial for assessing the profitability and financial stability of your notary business. Analyze key financial ratios and performance indicators, such as gross profit margin, net profit margin, and return on investment, to evaluate your business's financial performance against industry benchmarks. This analysis provides insights into your business's strengths and weaknesses, allowing you to make informed decisions and implement strategies for improvement.

Finally, consider engaging the services of a certified public accountant (CPA) or financial advisor to provide expert guidance on complex financial matters, tax planning, and long-term financial strategies. A professional with specialized knowledge can help you navigate the intricacies of financial management, maximize your profitability, and ensure compliance with financial regulations.

Accounting and financial management are integral to the success of notary businesses. By establishing robust financial systems, separating personal and business finances, maintaining accurate records, budgeting effectively, monitoring cash flow, complying with tax regulations, and conducting regular financial analysis, you can position your notary business for growth and profitability. Prioritizing sound financial practices demonstrates professionalism, instills client confidence, and lays the foundation for a sustainable and thriving business.

Setting up a business bank account for appropriate financial management

Setting up a business bank account is a critical step in establishing and maintaining proper financial management for your notary business. By creating a clear separation between your personal and business finances, you can effectively track and manage your business transactions, ensuring accuracy and facilitating efficient financial decision-making.

When selecting a bank for your business account, it is important to consider several factors that will impact your financial management. Begin by researching different banks and comparing their offerings, including reputation, available business banking services, fees, and convenience. Take the time to assess which bank aligns best with your business needs and objectives.

To initiate the process of opening a business bank account, gather the required documentation, such as your business registration documents (e.g., Articles of Organization or Certificate of Incorporation), your Employer Identification Number (EIN), and proof of identification for authorized signatories. These documents will demonstrate the legitimacy of your business and provide the necessary information for the bank to proceed with the account setup.

Once you have compiled the required documentation, schedule an appointment with the chosen bank to meet with a representative. During this meeting, you will complete the necessary forms and provide the requested documentation. The bank representative will guide you through the account opening process, explaining the various account options available, such as checking accounts, savings accounts, or specialized business accounts. This personalized guidance will help you select the account that best suits your specific business requirements.

When setting up your business bank account, consider the following factors:

1. Account Type:

Choose an account type that aligns with your business's financial needs and goals. A checking account allows for convenient day-to-day transactions, while a savings account may be beneficial for setting aside funds for taxes or future business investments.

2. Account Features:

Evaluate the features and services provided by the bank, such as online banking, mobile banking, and bill payment options. Robust online and mobile banking platforms can streamline financial management tasks and provide greater convenience for monitoring and controlling your business finances.

3. Fees and Charges:

Familiarize yourself with the fee structure associated with the business bank account. Assess any monthly maintenance fees, transaction fees, ATM fees, or other charges that may apply. Understanding the fee structure will help you choose a bank that offers competitive rates and aligns with your budget.

4. Additional Services:

Consider whether the bank offers additional services tailored to businesses, such as business credit cards, lines of credit, or merchant services. These supplementary offerings can provide valuable resources to support your business growth and financial needs.

After your business bank account is established, it is crucial to use it exclusively for business-related transactions. Mixing personal and business expenses can lead to confusion, inaccurate financial records, and potential tax complications. By maintaining a clear separation, you can effectively track and manage your business finances, ensuring accurate reporting and facilitating financial analysis.

Regularly monitor your business bank account for any unauthorized transactions or discrepancies. Stay vigilant and promptly address any issues or errors that may arise. Regular reconciliations of your bank statements with your financial records will help identify and rectify any discrepancies, ensuring the accuracy and integrity of your financial information.

Establishing a business bank account is an integral part of effective financial management for your notary business. By separating personal and business finances, you can track and manage your business transactions accurately. Research different banks and consider their offerings to find the most suitable option for your business needs. Once your account is set up, use it exclusively for business-related transactions, monitor it regularly, and reconcile your records to ensure accuracy and financial integrity.

Developing a bookkeeping system to track income and expenses

Developing a bookkeeping system is an essential aspect of business setup and administration. It involves keeping track of all financial transactions, including costs and payments. A well-designed bookkeeping system helps ensure the finances are properly managed, thus enabling informed decision-making.

The first step in developing a bookkeeping system is organizing all relevant financial documents, such as bank statements, receipts, and invoices. It ensures that no transaction goes unrecorded or unnoticed.

Once the papers are organized, choose a method for recording transactions- whether manual or electronic. The choice should base on factors such as the size of the business and available resources.

After selecting the recording method, it's time to set up categories for different types of income and expenses. Organizing these categories enables easy tracking of cash flow and identifying areas where adjustments require.

Establishing regular review periods - daily/weekly/monthly - helps keep track of trends in cash flow patterns over time. This information can help identify potential problems before they escalate into more significant issues affecting overall business performance.

Developing a sound bookkeeping system is critical in managing finances effectively during business setup and administration.

Implementing accounting software or hiring an accountant to handle finances

Implementing accounting software or hiring an accountant to manage finances is crucial when setting up and administering a business. As a business owner, it's important to track income and expenses accurately, so you can make informed financial decisions that drive growth.

By implementing accounting software like QuickBooks or Xero, you can quickly enter transactions, reconcile accounts and generate financial statements. It not only saves your time but minimizes errors in calculations.

However, if managing finances isn't your forte or if you prefer to have someone oversee your finances for you, then consider hiring an accountant. An experienced accountant can help ensure compliance with tax laws and regulations while providing valuable insights into the business's overall health.

When choosing between implementing accounting software or hiring an accountant, consider factors such as cost-effectiveness, the scope of work required for bookkeeping duties, and the level of expertise needed for management services.

You can check what is best for your specific business needs. Implementing accounting software is an excellent idea if you want to check everything on your finances without spending too much. But if you need more time and deal with complex finances, hiring an expert may be necessary.

Developing a robust bookkeeping system is essential for effectively tracking the income and expenses of your notary business. By establishing a solid financial foundation, you can ensure accurate record-keeping, make informed business decisions, and fulfill your tax obligations.

To start, consider the following steps in developing an effective bookkeeping system:

1. Choose an Accounting Method:

Select an accounting method that suits your business needs. The two primary methods are cash basis accounting and accrual basis accounting. Cash basis accounting records transactions when cash is received or paid, while accrual basis accounting records transactions when they are incurred, regardless of cash flow. Consult with an accountant to determine which method is most appropriate for your business.

2. Set up a Chart of Accounts:

A chart of accounts organizes your income and expense categories. It provides a structured framework for classifying and tracking your financial transactions. Common accounts include income accounts, expense accounts, asset accounts, liability accounts, and equity accounts. Customize your chart of accounts to align with the specific needs and structure of your notary business.

3. Establish a Record-Keeping System:

Determine how you will record and store your financial documents and data. Consider using accounting software, such as QuickBooks or Xero, which offer user-friendly interfaces and automated features for tracking income and expenses. These software solutions allow you to generate financial reports, reconcile bank statements, and streamline your bookkeeping processes.

4. Track Income:

Record all sources of income generated by your notary business. This includes notary fees, loan signing fees, and any additional services provided. Ensure that each transaction is accurately documented, including the date, client information, type of service performed, and payment received.

5. Record Expenses:

Maintain a detailed record of all business-related expenses. This includes office supplies, marketing expenses, professional development costs, insurance premiums, and any other expenditures incurred in the operation of your notary business. Retain receipts and invoices for each expense to support accurate record-keeping.

6. Reconcile Bank Statements:

Regularly reconcile your business bank statements with your bookkeeping records. This process ensures that all transactions are accurately recorded and any discrepancies are identified and resolved promptly. Reconciliation helps maintain the integrity of your financial data and provides a clear overview of your cash flow.

7. Create Financial Reports:

Utilize your bookkeeping system to generate financial reports, such as profit and loss statements, balance sheets, and cash flow statements. These reports provide valuable insights into the financial health of your notary business, allowing you to monitor revenue, track expenses, and assess overall profitability.

8. Seek Professional Guidance:

Consider consulting with an accountant or bookkeeping professional to ensure compliance with tax regulations, maximize deductions, and receive guidance on financial management best practices. An expert can offer valuable insights and assist with complex financial matters, enabling you to focus on the core aspects of your notary business.

Remember to maintain consistency and accuracy in your bookkeeping practices. Regularly update your records, review financial reports, and analyze key performance indicators to assess the financial health of your notary business. By developing a strong bookkeeping system, you will have a solid foundation for informed decision-making, tax compliance, and long-term success.

In implementing an effective bookkeeping system, it is crucial to customize it to meet your specific business needs and stay organized throughout the process. By following these steps and maintaining meticulous records, you can establish a reliable bookkeeping system that provides you with the financial information necessary to make informed business decisions and maintain the financial health of your notary business.

Creating a budget and monitoring cash flow

Creating a budget and monitoring cash flow is vital for the success of any business. It allows you to understand the track of your income and business clearly. This way, you can run your business well.

When creating a budget, start by listing all potential sources of income. It could include sales revenue, investments, or loans. Then list all expected expenses, such as rent, utilities, and salaries. Be sure to have fixed costs (those that do not change) and variable costs (those that fluctuate).

Once you have established your budget, it's essential to monitor it regularly. Use an accounting software or spreadsheet program to keep accurate records of income and expenses. It will let you overview whether you are meeting financial goals or if adjustments need to make.

Monitoring cash flow is also crucial for staying on top of finances. Cash flow uses the movement of money in and out of your business over time. Keeping track ensures that there are no surprises when bills come due.

Create projections based on historical data and expected future transactions to keep tabs on cash flow. Doing so lets you anticipate shortfalls in cash before they occur and take steps to remedy them.

Creating a budget and monitoring cash flow are critical components of effective financial management for your notary business. By establishing a budget and closely monitoring your cash flow, you can maintain control over your expenses, identify potential financial challenges, and make informed decisions to support the growth and profitability of your business.

1. Develop a Budget:

Creating a budget involves forecasting and allocating funds for different aspects of your notary business. Start by estimating your expected income for a specific period, such as a month or a year. This can include projected notary fees, loan signing fees, and any other sources of revenue. Next, identify your fixed expenses, such as office rent, utilities, insurance premiums, and software subscriptions. Consider variable expenses like marketing and advertising costs, professional development, and office supplies. Allocate appropriate funds for each category and ensure that your projected income covers your expenses. Regularly review and update your budget to reflect changes in your business.

2. Monitor Cash Flow:

Cash flow refers to the movement of money in and out of your business over a given period. Monitoring your cash flow involves tracking your incoming and outgoing cash transactions to ensure a healthy financial position. Start by tracking your cash inflows, which include payments from clients, loan signings, and any other sources of income. Simultaneously, record your cash outflows, such as rent, utilities, salaries, marketing expenses, and other operational costs. By maintaining accurate records of your cash flow, you can gain visibility into how funds are being utilized and make adjustments as necessary.

3. Implement Cash Flow Management Strategies:

To effectively manage cash flow, consider implementing the following strategies:

a) **Invoice Promptly:** Send out invoices promptly after providing services to clients to ensure timely payment. Clearly outline your payment terms and follow up on overdue invoices to expedite cash collection.

b) **Control Expenses:** Monitor your expenses closely and identify areas where you can reduce costs without compromising the quality of your services. Negotiate contracts with vendors, seek competitive pricing, and explore cost-effective alternatives.

c) **Manage Accounts Receivable:** Keep a close eye on outstanding payments and follow up with clients to ensure timely collection. Implement clear credit policies and consider offering incentives for early payments.

d) **Plan for Seasonal Variations:** If your notary business experiences seasonal fluctuations, plan ahead by setting aside funds during peak periods to cover expenses during slower periods. This will help maintain a consistent cash flow throughout the year.

e) **Establish Emergency Reserves:** Build a financial cushion by setting aside funds for unexpected expenses or emergencies. This will provide stability and peace of mind during challenging times.

4. Regularly Review Financial Reports:

Reviewing financial reports, such as cash flow statements, profit and loss statements, and balance sheets, is crucial for gaining insights into your business's financial performance. These reports provide an overview of your revenue, expenses, and overall profitability. Analyze trends, identify areas for improvement, and make informed decisions based on the information presented.

5. Seek Professional Assistance:

Consider engaging the services of an accountant or financial advisor to assist you in creating and managing your budget, as well as monitoring your cash flow. They can provide valuable insights, help you interpret financial reports, and offer guidance on financial planning and decision-making.

By creating a budget and closely monitoring your cash flow, you can proactively manage the financial aspects of your notary business. This will enable you to make informed decisions, identify potential issues before they arise, and ensure the long-term success and profitability of your business. Regularly assess and adjust your budget and cash flow management strategies to reflect changes in your business and market conditions. With careful financial management, you can navigate challenges, seize opportunities, and achieve your business goals.

Understanding and complying with financial reporting obligations

Running a business involves more than just setting up a bank account and keeping track of income and expenses. As an entrepreneur, you must comply with financial reporting obligations. It includes preparing regular financial statements, filing tax returns, and adhering to business regulations.

Understanding these requirements can be overwhelming for some entrepreneurs unfamiliar with accounting practices. However, seeking professional guidance or educating yourself on the basics of financial reporting is crucial. Doing so will help you avoid penalties and legal consequences while ensuring that your books accurately reflect your company's financial health.

Setting up a successful business requires careful planning and understanding each detail in all aspects of administration.

Understanding and complying with financial reporting obligations is crucial for maintaining the financial transparency and integrity of your notary business. Financial reporting involves the preparation and presentation of financial statements that accurately reflect your business's financial performance and position. Adhering to these obligations ensures compliance with legal and regulatory requirements and provides stakeholders, such as lenders, investors, and tax authorities, with essential information about your business's financial health.

1. Familiarize Yourself with Applicable Standards:

Start by understanding the financial reporting standards and regulations relevant to your notary business. In most jurisdictions, businesses are required to adhere to generally accepted accounting principles (GAAP) or international financial reporting standards (IFRS). These standards provide guidelines on the preparation, presentation, and disclosure of financial statements. Stay updated on any changes or updates to these standards to ensure compliance.

2. Prepare Financial Statements:

Financial statements are the primary documents used to communicate your business's financial performance to external parties. The key financial statements include:

a) **Income Statement (or Profit and Loss Statement):** This statement summarizes your revenue, expenses, and net income (or loss) for a specific period. It provides insights into your business's profitability.

b) **Balance Sheet:** The balance sheet provides a snapshot of your business's assets, liabilities, and equity at a particular point in time. It showcases your business's financial position.

c) **Cash Flow Statement:** This statement outlines the inflows and outflows of cash during a specific period. It helps analyze the sources and uses of cash within your business.

d) **Statement of Changes in Equity:** This statement tracks changes in your business's equity, including contributions, distributions, and retained earnings.

Prepare these financial statements in accordance with the applicable accounting standards and ensure they accurately reflect your business's financial performance and position.

3. Maintain Accurate Financial Records:

To fulfill your financial reporting obligations, it's essential to maintain accurate and organized financial records. Keep detailed records of your business transactions, including sales, expenses, assets, and liabilities. Use accounting software or engage the services of an accountant to ensure proper bookkeeping. Accurate financial records form the foundation for preparing reliable financial statements and facilitate compliance with reporting requirements.

4. Comply with Tax Reporting Obligations:

In addition to general financial reporting, ensure compliance with tax reporting obligations specific to your jurisdiction. Understand the tax laws governing your notary business, including income tax, sales tax, and any other applicable taxes. Keep track of tax deadlines, file accurate and timely tax returns, and maintain records to support your tax filings.

5. Engage Professional Assistance:

Consider working with an accountant or financial advisor who specializes in small businesses or notary services. They can provide guidance on financial reporting requirements, assist in the preparation of financial statements, and ensure compliance with regulations. Additionally, they can help interpret financial data, provide strategic insights, and assist in tax planning.

6. Regularly Review and Analyze Financial Reports:

Financial reports are not only for compliance purposes but also serve as valuable tools for monitoring and evaluating your business's financial performance. Regularly review your financial statements to gain insights into revenue trends, cost structures, and areas for improvement. Analyze key financial ratios, such as profitability, liquidity, and solvency, to assess your business's financial health and identify potential risks or opportunities.

Remember that financial reporting is an ongoing process. Continuously monitor changes in regulations, update your financial records, and review and adjust your reporting practices as needed. By understanding and complying with financial reporting obligations, you demonstrate transparency, maintain stakeholder confidence, and support the long-term success of your notary business.

By following the steps outlined above for accounting and financial management, you can establish a strong foundation for your new venture while minimizing risks associated with regulatory compliance. Remember that seeking expert advice when needed can save you time, money, and stress – ultimately contributing to long-term success.

Record Keeping and Document Management

A notary business must establish a system for organizing and storing important documents. It begins with designating a dedicated physical space or filing cabinet to keep physical records. A specific area for document storage allows you to locate and retrieve essential papers quickly.

Creating a logical and consistent file naming convention will enhance organization and efficiency. Categorizing documents based on their types, such as client agreements, notarial certificates, identification records, and other relevant categories, will make it easier to locate specific documents when required.

Consider using digital document management systems or cloud storage solutions for electronic files. These tools allow for efficient storage, retrieval, and backup of electronic documents, ensuring they are easily accessible while maintaining security.

Maintaining records of notarial acts performed and related documentation is crucial for a notary business.

It is essential to keep the whole narrative of each notarial act performed. It includes documenting the date, parties involved, the nature of the document, and any fees collected. Retaining copies of the notarized documents is equally important. Ensure that these copies are legible, adequately identified, and securely stored. One approach is establishing a logbook or digital database to record all notarial acts. This logbook should capture relevant details for future reference and tracking. By diligently maintaining these records, you will have a comprehensive and accurate account of your notarial activities, which can be helpful for legal and administrative purposes.

Proper data security measures are critical for protecting sensitive information in a notary business. Safeguarding client data and other confidential information is paramount.

If you want to save the confidentiality and accuracy of the documents you work with, utilizing physical and digital security measures is recommended. Physical security measures may include storing physical documents in locked cabinets or rooms accessible only to authorized personnel.

For electronic records, implement strong access controls, such as unique user accounts and passwords, to restrict access to sensitive information. Regularly update security software and protocols to guard against cyber threats. Additionally, consider encrypting sensitive digital files and backing up data regularly to prevent loss. Adhering to best practices in data security will help maintain client trust and protect your business from potential legal and reputational risks.

Understanding and complying with document retention and disposal requirements is vital for a notary business.

Different jurisdictions may have specific regulations regarding how long certain documents must retain. Familiarize yourself with these requirements to ensure compliance. Develop a document retention policy outlining the retention periods for various records.

This policy should remain the same for the disposal of the documents which are no longer required to retain. Implement a safe and consistent document disposal process, such as shredding physical documents or securely deleting electronic files, to protect client confidentiality and prevent unauthorized access to sensitive information.

You demonstrate professionalism and maintain legal compliance in your notary business by adhering to document retention and disposal requirements.

Liability Protection and Insurance

Assessing the liability risks associated with the notary business is an essential first step. As a notary, you must perform your duties accurately and ethically. However, errors or omissions in the notarial acts can occur, leading to potential liability issues. It's essential to identify the specific risks that your business may face. It could include errors in document preparation, improper identification verification, or failure to follow proper procedures. By conducting a thorough assessment, you can understand the potential liabilities and take appropriate measures to mitigate them.

Considering the primary business liability and insurance coverage options is crucial for protecting your notary business. General liability insurance is essential to save you from third-party claims, such as bodily injury or property damage, that may occur during your business activities. It will provide financial protection in unexpected lawsuits or claims against your business.

Additionally, professional liability insurance, also known as errors and omissions (E&O) insurance, is specifically designed for professionals who provide services, such as notaries. It can help cover legal expenses and damages from alleged errors, negligence, or omissions in your professional services. Evaluating different insurance providers and policies is essential to ensure they meet your notary business's specific needs and requirements.

Exploring professional liability insurance specific to notary services is highly recommended. Notarial acts involve dealing with legal documents and certifications, making professional liability coverage tailored to notaries a valuable investment. This type of insurance typically includes a range of errors or omissions in notarial acts, failure to follow proper procedures, and other related risks. Notary-specific professional liability insurance can provide financial protection if a client alleges that your services caused economic loss or harm. As notary regulations and requirements may vary across jurisdictions, choosing an insurance policy that aligns with the precise rules and regulations applicable to your practice is essential.

Evaluating the need for additional insurance, such as general liability or property insurance, is also necessary. Public liability insurance covers accidents or injuries at your premises or during business-related activities. This coverage can help protect against bodily injury, property damage, or personal injury claims. Property insurance is essential if you own or lease a physical office or space for your notary business. It covers losing your business property, including office equipment, furniture, and other assets. Evaluating your business operations and investments will help determine if additional insurance coverage is necessary to protect your notary business against potential risks and liabilities.

Taxes and Tax Planning

Registering for an Employer Identification Number (EIN) for your notary business is necessary. This EIN is a unique identification number issued by a relevant authority like Internal Revenue Service (IRS) to track your business for tax purposes. It is necessary when filing tax returns, hiring employees, opening business bank accounts, and conducting other financial transactions. Obtaining an EIN is typically a straightforward process and can do online through the IRS website.

Understanding and complying with tax obligations for the chosen business structure is crucial. The tax obligations for a notary business will depend on the selected business structure, such as a sole proprietorship, partnership, or LLC. It's essential to familiarize yourself with the tax requirements specific to your business structure. It includes understanding the different types of taxes you may be subject to, such as income tax, self-employment tax, and any applicable state or local taxes. Complying with tax obligations involves keeping accurate records of income, expenses, and deductions and meeting reporting and payment deadlines.

Keeping track of deductible expenses for tax purposes is essential for minimizing tax liabilities. As a notary business owner, you can deduct certain expenses related to your business operations. It can include office rent, equipment, supplies, professional development, and marketing costs. Maintaining thorough records and receipts of these expenses will help support your deductions and reduce your taxable income, lowering your tax liability.

Filing tax returns on time and paying applicable taxes are critical to complying with tax laws. As a notary business owner, you are required to file your tax returns by the specified deadlines. It includes reporting your business income, deductions, and other information needed. Also, paying applicable taxes, such as income or self-employment tax, is essential on time to avoid penalties and interest charges. Staying organized, keeping track of deadlines, and seeking professional assistance if needed can help ensure timely and accurate tax filing.

Exploring tax planning strategies is advisable to minimize your tax liabilities and optimize your financial position. Tax planning involves:

Reviewing your financial situation.

Understanding the tax laws.

Identifying legal opportunities to reduce your tax burden.

It may include strategies such as maximizing deductible expenses, taking advantage of available tax credits, structuring your business tax-efficiently, and utilizing retirement plans or other tax-advantaged savings options. You can consult a tax consultant to get insights. He can guide you well.

In conclusion, setting up and administering a notary business involves several crucial aspects that require careful attention. Choosing the appropriate business structure and selecting a unique and meaningful name lay the foundation for your business identity. Obtaining the necessary licenses and permits ensures legal compliance and allows you to operate your notary business within the boundaries of the law. Implementing practical accounting and financial management practices will help you in every aspect, like income, expenses, and budgets, enabling you to make informed financial decisions. A robust record-keeping and document management system ensures the organization, accessibility, and security of important documents and records. Protecting your business and personal assets through liability protection and insurance protects you from potential risks and liabilities arising from your notarial acts. Lastly, understanding your tax obligations, utilizing deductions, and exploring tax planning strategies can help optimize your tax position and minimize tax liabilities. By diligently addressing these areas, you can establish a solid foundation for your notary business and achieve success.

Chapter 5

The Art of Loan Signing

As a loan signer, you have a crucial role in assisting borrowers in obtaining their desired homes. This profession entails various responsibilities, such as comprehending the intricacies of mortgage loans and effectively handling challenging signers. This chapter will provide comprehensive information about loan signing, equipping you with the knowledge necessary to thrive in your role.

Understanding How Mortgage Loans Work

Mortgage loans are loans used to purchase real estate properties. They are typically long-term loans, with 15 to 30 years of repayment periods. When taking out a loan, you must understand that you will also be answerable for paying interest on the amount borrowed. This interest is typically charged as a percentage of the total amount borrowed and can add up over time. It's important to factor in the interest cost when determining if a loan is the right choice for your financial situation. I bot is a must that the borrower is bound to pay interest charges on the loan payments, which will charge as a percentage of the total borrowed.

The key parties involved in a mortgage transaction include:

- The lender (it can be a bank or financial institution).
- The borrower (the person taking out the loan).
- Sometimes an intermediary such as a mortgage broker.

Once approved for a mortgage loan, borrowers must sign several legal documents. These documents include promissory notes and deeds of trust or mortgages. A promissory letter outlines how much money was borrowed and how it will pay back over time. An act of trust or mortgage secures that debt with collateral - usually the home being purchased.

Before closing on a mortgage loan, borrowers receive various disclosures, including Loan Estimates and Closing Disclosures that outline all costs associated with their new home purchase. Additionally, they must review Truth-in-Lending Act (TILA) disclosures which provide additional information about interest rates and fees.

Understanding how mortgage loans work is essential for any loan signing agent. As a professional in the mortgage industry, you will be facilitating the signing of loan documents, and having a solid grasp of the mortgage loan process will enhance your effectiveness and confidence in your role.

Mortgage loans are a common form of financing used by individuals and families to purchase real estate. They involve a lender providing funds to a borrower in exchange for a lien on the property being purchased. Let's dive deeper into the key aspects of understanding how mortgage loans work.

1. Types of Mortgage Loans:

There are various types of mortgage loans available, including conventional loans, government-backed loans (such as FHA, VA, and USDA loans), adjustable-rate mortgages (ARMs), and fixed-rate mortgages. Each type has its own features, eligibility requirements, and terms. Familiarize yourself with these different loan types to better assist borrowers in understanding their options.

2. Mortgage Loan Process:

The mortgage loan process involves several stages, including pre-approval, application, underwriting, closing, and post-closing. It's important to understand each stage and the documents involved to effectively guide borrowers through the process.

a) **Pre-approval:** Before borrowers start house hunting, they often seek pre-approval from a lender. Pre-approval involves a lender reviewing the borrower's financial information and issuing a conditional commitment for a loan amount.

b) **Application:** Once borrowers find a property, they submit a loan application to the lender. The application includes personal and financial information, employment details, and the property's information.

c) **Underwriting:** During underwriting, the lender assesses the borrower's creditworthiness and verifies the information provided. They evaluate the borrower's income, credit history, assets, and liabilities to determine if they meet the loan requirements.

d) **Closing:** The closing is the final step where the loan documents are signed, and funds are disbursed to complete the purchase. As a loan signing agent, you play a crucial role in facilitating this process, ensuring all documents are signed accurately and in compliance with applicable laws.

3. Key Mortgage Loan Documents:

Being familiar with the various mortgage loan documents is essential. Some common documents you may encounter include:

a) **Loan Estimate (LE):** The LE provides borrowers with an estimate of the loan terms, including interest rate, fees, and closing costs.
b) **Closing Disclosure (CD):** The CD provides borrowers with the final details of the loan, including the loan terms, closing costs, and other important information.
c) **Promissory Note:** The promissory note is a legal document that outlines the borrower's promise to repay the loan. It includes details such as the loan amount, interest rate, repayment terms, and consequences for default.
d) **Deed of Trust (or Mortgage):** This document creates a lien on the property being financed. It outlines the borrower's obligations and the rights of the lender in case of default.

4. Interest Rates and Repayment Terms:

Understanding how interest rates and repayment terms impact the cost of borrowing is crucial. Interest rates determine the amount of interest borrowers will pay over the life of the loan. Repayment terms, such as the loan term (e.g., 15 or 30 years) and the frequency of payments (e.g., monthly), affect the borrower's monthly payment amount.

5. Loan Costs and Fees:

Educate yourself on the various costs and fees associated with mortgage loans. These may include origination fees, appraisal fees, title fees, and closing costs. Understanding these costs will enable you to explain them to borrowers and ensure transparency throughout the loan process.

6. Loan Servicing and Potential Changes:

Explain to borrowers the concept of loan servicing and the possibility of their loan being sold or transferred to another servicer.

Inform them about the importance of reviewing their loan statements, contacting the servicer for any questions or concerns, and understanding the terms of their loan.

As a loan signing agent, developing a comprehensive understanding of how mortgage loans work is vital. This knowledge will enable you to confidently guide borrowers through the loan process, explain key terms and documents, and ensure a smooth and successful closing experience. By continuously expanding your knowledge of mortgage loans, you position yourself as a trusted professional in the industry.

Key parties involved in a mortgage transaction

A mortgage transaction involves several key parties, each playing an essential role. Firstly, the borrower seeks a loan to purchase or refinance their property. Secondly, the lender provides funds to the borrower against the security of the property's title. The third party involved in this transaction includes real estate agents and brokers who help borrowers find suitable properties and lenders for financing.

The fourth important player in a mortgage transaction is a loan officer or underwriter responsible for reviewing and approving loan applications and verifying all supporting documents borrowers provide, such as credit reports and income statements. Additionally, appraisers are crucial as they determine the value of properties financed through mortgage loans.

Attorneys must ensure that all legal requirements for transferring property ownership from seller to buyer are met during closing transactions. At the same time, escrow agents act on behalf of both buyers and sellers during this final stage of completing a sale. Numerous parties come together throughout a typical mortgage transaction, making it essential for everyone involved to communicate effectively to ensure every step goes smoothly without any hiccups.

In a mortgage transaction, several key parties come together to facilitate the process. Understanding the roles and responsibilities of each party is essential for a loan signing agent to effectively navigate the complexities of the mortgage industry. Let's delve into the primary parties involved in a mortgage transaction:

1. Borrower:

The borrower, also known as the mortgagor, is an individual or entity seeking financing to purchase a property. They initiate the loan process by submitting an application, providing financial information, and ultimately assume the responsibility of repaying the loan.

2. Lender:

The lender, also referred to as the mortgagee, is the financial institution or entity providing the funds to the borrower. Lenders can include banks, credit unions, mortgage companies, or even private individuals. They assess the borrower's creditworthiness, evaluate the loan application, and make the decision to approve or deny the loan.

3. Loan Officer:

A loan officer works for the lender and serves as the main point of contact for borrowers throughout the loan process. They assist borrowers in completing the loan application, gather necessary documentation, and guide them through the underwriting process.

4. Loan Processor:

The loan processor works behind the scenes, ensuring that all required documentation is complete and accurate. They verify the borrower's information, order necessary reports (such as credit reports and property appraisals), and prepare the loan file for underwriting.

5. Underwriter:

The underwriter assesses the borrower's creditworthiness and evaluates the loan application in line with the lender's guidelines. They review the borrower's financial documents, employment history, credit report, and property appraisal to determine if the loan meets the lender's risk criteria.

6. Appraiser:

An appraiser plays a crucial role in the mortgage process by determining the market value of the property being financed. They conduct a thorough assessment of the property's condition, location, and comparable sales in the area to provide an unbiased estimate of its value.

7. Title Company:

The title company ensures that the property's title is clear and can be transferred to the borrower without any legal issues. They conduct a title search, obtain title insurance, and facilitate the closing process by preparing the necessary documents.

8. Escrow Officer:

The escrow officer, typically employed by the title company or an independent escrow company, acts as a neutral third party in the transaction. They handle the transfer of funds and documents between the parties involved, ensuring that all conditions of the loan are met before the closing.

9. Loan Signing Agent:

The loan signing agent, a critical participant in the mortgage transaction, facilitates the signing of loan documents. They ensure that borrowers understand the documents they are signing, collect any required signatures or initials, and notarize the relevant documents.

10. Real Estate Agent:

Although not directly involved in the loan process, real estate agents play a significant role in connecting borrowers with lenders and assisting with property purchases. They help borrowers find suitable properties, negotiate offers, and provide guidance throughout the home-buying process.

Each of these parties plays a unique role in a mortgage transaction, and their collaboration ensures a smooth and successful closing. As a loan signing agent, understanding the responsibilities and interactions among these key players allows you to navigate the process with professionalism and efficiency. By fostering strong relationships with these parties, you can enhance your reputation and establish yourself as a trusted partner in the mortgage industry.

Types of Mortgage Documents You Will Sign

As a loan signing agent, you will encounter various types of mortgage documents that borrowers are required to sign during the loan closing process. Familiarizing yourself with these documents is crucial to ensure a smooth and accurate signing experience. Let's explore some of the key types of mortgage documents you may encounter:

1. Mortgage Note:

The mortgage note, also known as the promissory note, is a legally binding agreement between the borrower and the lender. It outlines the terms of the loan, including the loan amount, interest rate, repayment schedule, and any applicable penalties or fees. By signing the mortgage note, the borrower acknowledges their obligation to repay the loan.

2. Deed of Trust (or Mortgage):

The deed of trust, or mortgage, is a document that establishes a lien on the property being financed. It provides the lender with the right to foreclose on the property in the event of default. The borrower signs this document to acknowledge the lender's security interest in the property.

3. Loan Estimate:

The loan estimate is a disclosure document provided to borrowers within three business days of applying for a mortgage. It outlines the estimated costs and terms of the loan, including the interest rate, closing costs, and monthly payment. Borrowers must carefully review and sign the loan estimate to indicate their understanding of the loan terms.

4. Closing Disclosure:

The closing disclosure is a detailed breakdown of the final terms and costs associated with the mortgage loan. It is provided to borrowers at least three business days before the scheduled closing date. The document includes information such as the loan amount, interest rate, closing costs, and loan terms. The borrower's signature confirms their receipt and understanding of the closing disclosure.

5. Truth in Lending Act (TILA) Disclosures:

Under the Truth in Lending Act, borrowers must receive certain disclosures related to the costs and terms of their mortgage loan. These disclosures include the Annual Percentage Rate (APR), finance charges, and other loan-specific details. As a loan signing agent, you may encounter documents such as the TILA disclosure statement or the Loan Estimate, which contain these required disclosures.

6. Affidavit of Occupancy:

An affidavit of occupancy is a document in which the borrower affirms that they intend to occupy the property as their primary residence. This document is commonly required for certain types of mortgage loans, such as those offered to owner-occupants.

7. Power of Attorney:

In some cases, borrowers may appoint a power of attorney (POA) to act on their behalf during the loan closing process. The POA document grants the designated individual the authority to sign the necessary loan documents on behalf of the borrower.

8. Insurance Documents:

Depending on the lender's requirements, borrowers may need to sign documents related to property insurance, such as proof of homeowners insurance or flood insurance, if applicable. These documents ensure that the property is adequately insured, protecting both the borrower and the lender's interests.

9. Additional Disclosures and Addendums:

Throughout the loan process, borrowers may be required to sign various additional disclosures and addendums. These could include documents related to the appraisal, title insurance, property condition, or any specific lender requirements.

It is essential as a loan signing agent to familiarize yourself with these types of mortgage documents and their significance in the loan process. Understanding the purpose and implications of each document allows you to guide borrowers through the signing process with confidence and professionalism. By ensuring that borrowers have a clear understanding of the documents they are signing, you contribute to a successful and compliant loan closing experience.

Promissory note

It means a legal document that determines the terms and conditions of a loan. It serves as evidence of debt and specifies the amount borrowed, interest rate, repayment schedule, and consequences for defaulting on the loan.

The person who signs the promissory note is the borrower or obligor. The lender or oblige holds onto this document until it's fully paid off. In other words, it represents a promise to repay money borrowed from someone else.

The promissory note sets out all essential details to ensure complete transparency between both parties involved in a mortgage transaction. It can be secured by collateral such as real estate property or unsecured with no security attached.

It also provides specific clauses that could lead to penalties if ignored by either party during signing; these may include late payment fees, prepayment penalties, or acceleration clauses, which accelerate payment schedules in case of a breach of contract.

With an understanding of what a promissory note entails, borrowers can have confidence when agreeing to loan request terms knowing they would avoid falling into financial difficulties down the line.

A critical document in the mortgage lending process is the promissory note. The promissory note serves as a legally binding agreement between the borrower and the lender, outlining the terms and conditions of the loan. Let's delve into the promissory note in more detail.

The promissory note is a written promise from the borrower to repay the loan amount to the lender. It contains important information, including:

1. Loan Details:

The promissory note includes essential loan details, such as the loan amount, interest rate, and repayment terms. It specifies whether the interest rate is fixed or adjustable and provides the repayment schedule, including the number of installments and their due dates. Additionally, it may outline any late payment penalties or fees.

2. Borrower's Obligations:

The promissory note clearly states the borrower's obligations in repaying the loan. It establishes the borrower's commitment to make timely payments, including the amount due, frequency, and duration. By signing the promissory note, the borrower acknowledges their responsibility to fulfill these obligations.

3. Lender's Rights:

The promissory note outlines the rights of the lender in case of default or breach of the loan agreement. It may include provisions allowing the lender to accelerate the loan, meaning they can demand immediate repayment of the entire outstanding balance in certain circumstances. The note may also detail the lender's rights to pursue legal action, including foreclosure, to recover the loan amount.

4. Prepayment Terms:

The promissory note may address prepayment options, providing clarity on whether the borrower can make early payments without incurring penalties or fees. It may outline any restrictions or conditions related to prepayment, giving borrowers an understanding of their options.

5. Collateral:

If the loan is secured by collateral, such as real estate, the promissory note may include provisions related to the collateral. It may specify the property's address, legal description, and any requirements related to insurance or maintenance.

6. Governing Law and Jurisdiction:

The promissory note often includes a section specifying the governing law and jurisdiction applicable to the loan agreement. This ensures that any disputes or legal matters related to the loan will be resolved according to the specified jurisdiction's laws.

The promissory note is a crucial document that sets the terms and conditions of the loan and establishes the legal relationship between the borrower and the lender. It serves as evidence of the borrower's commitment to repay the loan and provides clarity on the lender's rights and remedies in case of default.

As a loan signing agent, understanding the promissory note is vital in guiding borrowers through the loan signing process. By explaining the terms and ensuring that borrowers comprehend their obligations, you contribute to a transparent and smooth loan closing experience. Your professionalism and attention to detail in handling the promissory note demonstrate your commitment to facilitating a successful transaction for both the borrower and the lender.

Deed of trust or mortgage

Another significant document in the mortgage process is the deed of trust or mortgage. This legal instrument serves as security for the repayment of the loan and provides the lender with an interest in the property. Let's delve into the deed of trust or mortgage in more detail.

The deed of trust or mortgage is a document that establishes a lien on the property, granting the lender the right to foreclose and sell the property in the event of default. Here are key points to understand about the deed of trust or mortgage:

1. Parties Involved:

The deed of trust or mortgage involves three parties: the borrower (also known as the mortgagor), the lender (also known as the mortgagee), and a neutral third party called the trustee. The trustee holds the legal title to the property on behalf of the lender until the loan is fully repaid.

2. Property Description:

The deed of trust or mortgage includes a detailed description of the property being used as collateral for the loan. This description typically includes the property's address, legal description, and any relevant identifying information.

3. Mortgage Terms:

The document outlines the terms of the mortgage, including the loan amount, interest rate, repayment schedule, and duration. It also states any conditions or provisions related to the loan, such as prepayment penalties or restrictions on transfer of ownership.

4. Lien on the Property:

By signing the deed of trust or mortgage, the borrower grants the lender a lien on the property. This means that the lender has a legal claim on the property until the loan is fully paid off. The lien provides the lender with security and recourse in case of default.

5. Foreclosure Process:

The deed of trust or mortgage specifies the process for foreclosure in case of loan default. It outlines the steps that the lender can take to initiate foreclosure proceedings, including the notice requirements and the timeline for foreclosure sale. The document also details the borrower's rights and opportunities to cure the default.

6. Release of Lien:

Once the loan is fully repaid, the lender releases the lien on the property by issuing a satisfaction of mortgage or reconveyance deed. This document acknowledges that the borrower has fulfilled their obligations, and the lender no longer has a claim on the property.

The deed of trust or mortgage plays a crucial role in protecting the lender's interests and ensuring repayment of the loan. As a loan signing agent, it is essential to explain the contents of the deed of trust or mortgage to borrowers, helping them understand their responsibilities and the consequences of default. By facilitating a clear and informed signing process, you contribute to a successful mortgage transaction.

Remember, the specific details and terminology of the deed of trust or mortgage may vary depending on the jurisdiction and the specific loan program. It is crucial to stay updated on local regulations and consult legal professionals when necessary to ensure compliance and accuracy in the loan signing process.

Loan estimate and closing disclosure

The Loan Estimate (LE) and Closing Disclosure are two critical documents in the mortgage process that provide borrowers with crucial information about their loan terms and associated costs. Let's explore these documents in detail and understand their significance.

The Loan Estimate serves as an initial disclosure provided by lenders to borrowers within three business days of receiving a loan application. This document provides borrowers with an overview of the loan terms, estimated interest rate, monthly payment, and closing costs. It includes essential information such as the loan amount, loan term, type of loan, and whether the interest rate or payment can change over time.

One of the primary purposes of the Loan Estimate is to help borrowers compare loan offers from different lenders. By standardizing the presentation of loan terms and costs, it enables borrowers to make informed decisions about the most suitable loan option for their needs. It also highlights any potential changes to the loan terms over the life of the loan, such as adjustments in interest rates or payments.

The Loan Estimate also itemizes the estimated closing costs, which include fees for various services involved in the mortgage process, such as appraisal, credit report, title insurance, and government recording charges. It provides borrowers with a breakdown of the costs they can expect to pay at closing, helping them anticipate and plan for these expenses. Understanding the closing costs is essential for borrowers to budget appropriately and avoid any surprises at the closing table.

Upon receiving the Loan Estimate, borrowers have ten business days to indicate their intent to proceed with the loan application. This timeframe allows them to review the terms and costs thoroughly and seek clarifications from the lender if needed. It is crucial for borrowers to take this opportunity to carefully evaluate the loan offer and consider other factors like their financial situation, long-term goals, and affordability.

Once the loan application progresses and the closing date approaches, the Closing Disclosure comes into play. The Closing Disclosure provides borrowers with the final loan terms, including the interest rate, monthly payment, closing costs, and loan amount. It serves as a detailed breakdown of the financial aspects of the mortgage transaction.

The Closing Disclosure is designed to ensure that borrowers are aware of any changes that may have occurred during the loan process and have ample time to review and address any concerns. It must be provided to borrowers at least three business days before the loan closing, allowing them sufficient time to go through the document and seek further clarification if needed.

Comparing the Closing Disclosure to the Loan Estimate is crucial for borrowers to verify the accuracy of the loan terms and ensure that there are no significant discrepancies or unexpected changes. If any inconsistencies or errors are identified, borrowers have the opportunity to raise concerns and address them with the lender or other involved parties.

As a loan signing agent, it is your responsibility to help borrowers understand the contents of both the Loan Estimate and the Closing Disclosure. You play a crucial role in ensuring transparency and clarity throughout the mortgage process. By explaining the terms, costs, and potential changes to borrowers, you empower them to make informed decisions and navigate the loan closing process with confidence.

It is important to stay updated with the regulations governing the Loan Estimate and Closing Disclosure, such as the Truth in Lending Act (TILA) and the Real Estate Settlement Procedures Act (RESPA). These regulations aim to protect consumers and promote fair and transparent lending practices. By familiarizing yourself with these regulations and staying informed about any updates or changes, you can ensure compliance and accuracy in the loan signing process.

In conclusion, the Loan Estimate and Closing Disclosure are crucial documents in the mortgage process that provide borrowers with vital information about their loan terms and associated costs.

As a loan signing agent, it is essential to help borrowers understand and navigate these documents, empowering them to make informed decisions and ensuring a smooth and transparent loan closing experience. By staying informed about the regulations governing these documents and maintaining clear communication with lenders and borrowers, you can play a valuable role in the mortgage industry.

Truth-in-Lending Act (TILA) disclosures

The Truth in Lending Act (TILA) is a federal law enacted to protect consumers in credit transactions by promoting the informed use of credit and ensuring transparency in lending practices. Under TILA, lenders are required to provide borrowers with certain disclosures that outline the terms, costs, and other important information related to the credit agreement. These disclosures play a crucial role in empowering borrowers to make informed decisions and understand the financial implications of the credit they are seeking.

One of the key TILA disclosures is the Loan Estimate, which we discussed earlier. The Loan Estimate provides borrowers with an overview of the loan terms and estimated costs associated with the mortgage transaction. It helps borrowers compare loan offers from different lenders and understand the financial implications of the loan.

Another important TILA disclosure is the Closing Disclosure. This document provides borrowers with the final terms and costs of the loan, including the interest rate, monthly payment, closing costs, and loan amount. The Closing Disclosure must be provided to borrowers at least three business days before the loan closing, giving them ample time to review and address any concerns.

TILA also requires lenders to provide borrowers with a disclosure statement known as the Annual Percentage Rate (APR) disclosure. The APR represents the cost of credit expressed as an annual interest rate and includes both the interest rate and certain finance charges associated with the loan. The APR disclosure helps borrowers compare the costs of different loan offers and understand the true cost of borrowing.

In addition to these disclosures, TILA requires lenders to provide borrowers with a statement known as the Total Finance Charge. This statement itemizes the total cost of credit over the life of the loan, including all interest and fees. The Total Finance Charge helps borrowers understand the overall cost of the loan and compare it to other loan options.

TILA also imposes requirements on advertising practices related to credit offers. Lenders must include certain key information, such as the APR, in their advertisements to ensure that consumers have access to accurate and meaningful information when evaluating credit offers.

Furthermore, TILA includes provisions for the right of rescission in certain types of credit transactions. This means that in certain cases, borrowers have the right to cancel or rescind the credit agreement within a specified timeframe, typically three business days. The right of rescission provides an important safeguard for borrowers, particularly in cases where they may have entered into a credit agreement hastily or without fully understanding the terms.

Compliance with TILA disclosures is essential for lenders to fulfill their legal obligations and protect consumers. Failure to provide accurate and timely disclosures can result in significant penalties and legal consequences for lenders. As a loan signing agent, it is crucial to familiarize yourself with TILA requirements and ensure that the necessary disclosures are provided to borrowers during the loan signing process.

The Truth in Lending Act (TILA) requires lenders to provide borrowers with important disclosures that outline the terms, costs, and other key information related to credit transactions. These disclosures, including the Loan Estimate, Closing Disclosure, APR disclosure, and Total Finance Charge statement, empower borrowers to make informed decisions and understand the true cost of credit. As a loan signing agent, it is important to ensure compliance with TILA requirements and assist borrowers in understanding these disclosures, thereby promoting transparency and consumer protection in the lending industry.

Other supporting documents (e.g., insurance forms, addendums)

In addition to the essential mortgage documents we have discussed, there are other supporting documents that may be involved in a loan signing transaction. These documents serve to provide additional information, clarify specific terms, or address specific contingencies related to the mortgage agreement. While the exact set of supporting documents can vary depending on the nature of the loan and the specific requirements of the lender, let's explore some common examples:

1. Insurance Forms:

Depending on the type of property being financed, borrowers may be required to provide proof of insurance coverage. This typically includes homeowners insurance or hazard insurance, which protects against damage to the property and liability in case of accidents. The insurance forms will detail the coverage amount, policy term, and the insurance company's contact information. These forms are important for the lender to ensure that the property is adequately protected against potential risks.

2. Addendums:

Addendums are supplementary documents that modify or add specific terms to the original loan agreement. They are used to address specific contingencies or clarify certain aspects of the transaction. For example, there may be an addendum related to repairs or improvements that need to be completed on the property before the loan is finalized. Addendums ensure that all parties involved in the transaction are aware of and agree to any additional terms or conditions.

3. Disclosures:

Various disclosures may be required to provide borrowers with specific information about the loan or the property. For example, there may be a flood zone disclosure if the property is located in a designated flood zone area. Other disclosures may include lead-based paint disclosures, which are necessary for properties built before 1978, or disclosures related to potential hazards or environmental concerns.

4. Verification of Employment and Income:

Lenders often require borrowers to provide documentation to verify their employment and income. This may include recent pay stubs, W-2 forms, or tax returns. These documents help lenders assess the borrower's ability to repay the loan and ensure that the income stated on the loan application is accurate.

5. Appraisal Reports:

An appraisal report is prepared by a licensed appraiser to determine the fair market value of the property. This document is important for the lender to ensure that the property's value aligns with the loan amount. The appraisal report provides an objective assessment of the property's worth based on various factors, including comparable sales in the area, condition of the property, and market trends.

6. Title Documents:

Title documents establish ownership and any potential liens or encumbrances on the property. These documents include the title deed, title insurance policy, and any related endorsements. They ensure that the lender has a valid and enforceable lien on the property and that there are no legal issues or disputes regarding ownership.

It is important for loan signing agents to be familiar with these supporting documents and understand their purpose in the mortgage transaction. While not all of these documents may be present in every loan signing, being knowledgeable about their existence and significance will help you provide a comprehensive and professional service to borrowers and ensure a smooth closing process.

By accurately reviewing, explaining, and collecting these supporting documents during the loan signing process, loan signing agents contribute to the overall efficiency and integrity of the transaction. Their expertise in handling these documents helps borrowers feel confident and well-informed, while also ensuring compliance with lender requirements and legal obligations.

Supporting documents such as insurance forms, addendums, disclosures, verification of employment and income, appraisal reports, and title documents play a vital role in the mortgage transaction. Loan signing agents must be well-versed in these documents to provide a seamless and professional service, enabling borrowers to have a clear understanding of their obligations and rights in the loan process. By diligently handling and explaining these supporting documents, loan signing agents contribute to a successful and efficient closing experience.

Strategies for Managing Common Signing Situations

When it comes to managing common signing situations as a loan signing agent, there are several strategies that can help you navigate potential challenges and ensure a smooth and successful signing process. These strategies involve effective communication, attention to detail, and proactive problem-solving. Let's explore some key strategies for managing common signing situations.

1. Preparing in Advance:

Before each signing appointment, it's essential to thoroughly review the loan documents and familiarize yourself with the specific signing requirements. This preparation allows you to anticipate any potential issues or questions that may arise during the signing and ensures you are well-equipped to handle them.

2. Clear Communication:

Effective communication is crucial throughout the signing process. This includes communicating clearly and professionally with the borrowers, answering any questions they may have, and providing clear instructions on how to complete the necessary documents. By establishing open lines of communication, you can build trust and confidence with the borrowers.

3. Attention to Detail:

As a loan signing agent, attention to detail is paramount. Take the time to carefully review each document during the signing, ensuring that all signatures, initials, and dates are completed accurately. Verify that all required notarizations are executed correctly, and double-check for any missing or incomplete information. Attention to detail helps prevent errors and ensures the integrity of the signing process.

4. Problem-Solving Skills:

In certain signing situations, unexpected challenges may arise. It's essential to approach these situations with a problem-solving mindset. This may involve working with the borrowers and the signing parties to find alternative solutions or seeking guidance from the appropriate parties, such as escrow officers or loan officers. Being proactive and resourceful in resolving issues can help maintain the signing's momentum and avoid unnecessary delays.

5. Professionalism and Customer Service:

Demonstrating professionalism and providing excellent customer service are key to managing signing situations effectively. Arrive punctually for each appointment, dressed appropriately and with all necessary tools and equipment. Maintain a calm and composed demeanor throughout the signing, addressing any concerns or questions with patience and empathy. Going the extra mile to ensure a positive experience for the borrowers can lead to client satisfaction and potential referrals.

6. Continuing Education:

The mortgage industry is continually evolving, with new loan programs, regulations, and documents being introduced. Stay updated on industry changes by investing in your professional development through ongoing education and training. This ensures that you are equipped with the latest knowledge and skills to handle various signing situations effectively.

7. Building a Support Network:

As a loan signing agent, it can be beneficial to connect with other professionals in the industry. Building relationships with escrow officers, title companies, and other loan signing agents can provide valuable insights, guidance, and support when managing challenging signing situations. Networking and participating in industry events or forums can help expand your support network.

By implementing these strategies, you can enhance your ability to manage common signing situations as a loan signing agent. Remember that each signing may present unique challenges, but by maintaining professionalism, clear communication, attention to detail, and a problem-solving mindset, you can navigate these situations successfully and provide exceptional service to your clients.

Handling challenging signers (e.g., borrowers with language barriers or disabilities)

Handling challenging signers, such as borrowers with language barriers or disabilities, requires patience, empathy, and adaptability as a loan signing agent. It's essential to approach these situations with sensitivity and professionalism to ensure that all parties involved can fully understand and participate in the signing process. Here are some strategies for effectively handling challenging signers:

1. Communication and Language Barriers:

When encountering borrowers with language barriers, it's crucial to establish effective communication channels. If possible, try to determine the preferred language of the borrowers in advance and consider arranging for a qualified interpreter to be present during the signing. This ensures accurate communication and comprehension of the loan documents. If an interpreter is not available, explore alternative communication methods, such as using translation apps or seeking assistance from a bilingual colleague. Maintain a patient and respectful demeanor throughout the signing, allowing additional time for clarification and ensuring that the borrowers feel comfortable asking questions.

2. Disabilities and Special Needs:

When working with borrowers who have disabilities or special needs, adaptability and accessibility are key. Take the time to understand the specific needs of the borrowers before the signing appointment. This may involve asking them about any accommodations they require, such as large-print documents, Braille materials, or sign language interpretation. Ensure that the signing location is accessible for individuals with mobility challenges. If necessary, collaborate with the borrowers or their caregivers to make any necessary adjustments to the signing process, allowing them to participate fully.

3. Patience and Empathy:

Challenging signers may require additional time and support during the signing process. Maintain a patient and understanding approach, demonstrating empathy and recognizing the unique circumstances they may be facing. Be prepared to answer questions and provide explanations in a clear and concise manner. Avoid rushing the signers and allow them sufficient time to review and understand each document before proceeding. By displaying patience and empathy, you create a more comfortable and inclusive environment for the borrowers.

4. Flexibility and Adaptability:

Each signer is unique, and their individual needs may vary. As a loan signing agent, it's essential to remain flexible and adaptable when working with challenging signers. Be prepared to modify your signing approach based on the specific requirements of each individual. This may involve adjusting the signing pace, using alternative communication methods, or employing assistive technologies to facilitate the process. By being flexible and adapting to the needs of the borrowers, you can ensure a more inclusive and accommodating signing experience.

5. Sensitivity to Cultural Differences:

In some cases, borrowers with language barriers may also have cultural differences that influence their signing experience. It's crucial to be aware of and sensitive to these cultural nuances. Respect their cultural practices and customs, and strive to create a welcoming and inclusive atmosphere. Take the time to explain any unfamiliar concepts or terms in a culturally sensitive manner, promoting understanding and trust.

6. Collaboration and Support:

In challenging signing situations, it can be helpful to collaborate with other professionals involved in the process. Engage with escrow officers, loan officers, or title company representatives to seek guidance and support. They may have experience working with similar signers and can provide valuable insights and assistance. By leveraging the expertise of others, you can navigate challenging signers more effectively.

Remember, handling challenging signers requires a compassionate and adaptable approach. By prioritizing effective communication, demonstrating patience and empathy, and being responsive to their unique needs, you can ensure that all borrowers, regardless of language barriers or disabilities, have a positive signing experience. Your professionalism and dedication to inclusivity contribute to the overall success of the signing process.

Dealing with missing or incorrect information on documents

Dealing with missing or incorrect information on documents is a common challenge that loan signing agents encounter during the mortgage loan signing process. As a professional in the field, it is essential to handle these situations with diligence and accuracy to ensure the integrity of the transaction. Here are strategies for effectively managing missing or incorrect information on documents:

1. Thorough Document Review:

Before the signing appointment, carefully review all the loan documents provided to you by the lender or title company. Pay close attention to the required fields, signatures, dates, and other pertinent information. Familiarize yourself with the specific requirements of each document to identify any potential gaps or errors. By conducting a thorough review beforehand, you can proactively address any issues that may arise during the signing.

2. Open Communication:

Establish open lines of communication with the borrowers, escrow officers, and other relevant parties involved in the transaction. Encourage borrowers to carefully review the documents and inform them that they should feel free to ask questions or raise concerns about any missing or incorrect information. Foster a supportive and collaborative environment where borrowers feel comfortable sharing their feedback. By promoting open communication, you can quickly identify and address any discrepancies.

3. Clarification and Verification:

When encountering missing or incorrect information, it is crucial to seek clarification and verification from the appropriate sources. Communicate with the borrowers and other parties involved to understand the intent behind the missing or incorrect information. Contact the lender or title company to verify any discrepancies and obtain the accurate information required to complete the documents. Maintain detailed records of the clarification process to ensure a thorough and accurate trail of communication.

4. Attention to Detail:

Pay meticulous attention to detail during the signing process to identify any missing or incorrect information. Double-check all fields, dates, and signatures to ensure their accuracy and completeness. If you notice any discrepancies, promptly address them with the borrowers and seek the necessary corrections. Avoid making assumptions or guessing the intended information; instead, rely on verified sources and documentation.

5. Document Amendments and Corrections:

In situations where missing or incorrect information is identified, work closely with the borrowers, lenders, and title companies to facilitate document amendments or corrections. Follow the specific instructions provided by the lender or title company for making corrections, ensuring that all necessary parties are involved in the process. Keep detailed records of the amendments or corrections made, including any additional signatures or notations required. Maintain a professional and organized approach to ensure the accuracy and validity of the documents.

6. Timely Resolution:

Addressing missing or incorrect information promptly is crucial to prevent delays in the loan closing process. Act swiftly to communicate the discrepancies to the appropriate parties and work collaboratively to resolve them as soon as possible. Maintain regular follow-up with the lenders or title companies to ensure that the necessary amendments or corrections are made in a timely manner. By prioritizing timely resolution, you contribute to the smooth flow of the transaction and maintain the confidence of all parties involved.

7. Documentation and Reporting:

Keep meticulous records of any missing or incorrect information encountered during the signing process. Document the steps taken to address the discrepancies, including all communication and resolutions made. This documentation serves as evidence of your diligent approach and provides a comprehensive record of the transaction. Should any questions or concerns arise in the future, these records will be invaluable in demonstrating your professionalism and adherence to protocols.

8. Continuous Education and Professional Development:

Stay updated on industry standards, best practices, and any changes to loan document requirements. Attend training sessions, workshops, and conferences to enhance your knowledge and skills in the field. By continuously educating yourself, you can better navigate the complexities of the loan signing process and proactively address any issues related to missing or incorrect information.

Effectively managing missing or incorrect information on loan documents requires attention to detail, open communication, and a proactive approach. By conducting thorough document reviews, fostering open lines of communication, seeking clarification and verification, and facilitating timely resolutions, you can ensure the accuracy and integrity of the loan signing process. Your professionalism and dedication to accuracy contribute to a successful and seamless transaction.

Resolving discrepancies or issues during the signing process

Resolving discrepancies or issues during the signing process is a crucial responsibility that falls upon the shoulders of a diligent and meticulous loan signing agent. Acting as the intermediary between borrowers, lenders, and other parties involved in the transaction, it is essential to handle these situations promptly and effectively. By employing strategic approaches, a skilled loan signing agent can navigate through these challenges with finesse and professionalism. Let's explore some strategies for effectively resolving discrepancies or issues during the signing process.

One of the first steps in addressing discrepancies is to identify them accurately. As you guide borrowers through the signing process, it is imperative to meticulously review each document, keeping a keen eye out for any potential discrepancies or issues. This involves thoroughly comparing the information on the documents with the borrower's details and the lender's instructions to ensure accuracy. Look for missing information, incorrect dates, inconsistencies in signatures, or any other potential errors that may arise.

In the face of discrepancies or issues, maintaining a professional and calm demeanor is paramount. It is crucial to approach the situation with a problem-solving mindset and reassure the borrowers that you are committed to resolving any concerns. By remaining composed and composed, you can instill confidence in the borrowers, creating an atmosphere of trust and cooperation.

Clear and effective communication plays a pivotal role in resolving discrepancies or issues during the signing process. It is essential to clearly explain the nature of the discrepancy to the borrowers, ensuring they have a comprehensive understanding of the situation. Using plain language and avoiding technical jargon can facilitate their comprehension. Encourage borrowers to ask questions and address any concerns they may have, fostering an environment of open and transparent communication throughout the process.

Collaboration with relevant parties may be necessary to resolve discrepancies. This could involve contacting the lender, title company, or escrow officer to clarify conflicting information or seek necessary corrections. Timely and proactive communication of the issue to the appropriate parties is crucial. By working together with the relevant stakeholders, a cooperative and collaborative approach can be fostered, leading to a smooth resolution process.

In situations where you encounter a discrepancy or issue that you are unsure how to address, seeking guidance from your professional network or industry resources can prove invaluable. Connecting with fellow loan signing agents, industry associations, or mentors who have encountered similar situations can provide valuable insights and guidance on how to effectively resolve the discrepancy.

Maintaining meticulous records throughout the signing process is essential. Documenting the steps taken to address discrepancies, including all communication, resolutions, and amendments made, serves as evidence of your proactive approach and ensures a comprehensive record of the transaction. Additionally, any significant issues or unresolved discrepancies should be reported to the appropriate parties or authorities as required.

Time is of the essence when it comes to resolving discrepancies or issues during the signing process. Acting promptly to communicate the discrepancy to the relevant parties and working towards a resolution within the specified timelines is crucial. Following up with the lender, title company, or other involved parties ensures that necessary amendments or corrections are made in a timely manner. By prioritizing timely resolution, you contribute to the efficiency and success of the transaction.

Throughout the process of resolving discrepancies or issues, it is crucial to maintain professionalism and uphold strict confidentiality. Respecting the privacy and confidentiality of the borrowers' information, handling all documents and discussions with utmost discretion, and maintaining a professional image are paramount. By conducting yourself in a manner that instills trust and confidence in all parties involved, you foster a positive and conducive environment for resolving discrepancies.

Resolving discrepancies or issues during the signing process demands attention to detail, effective communication, and a proactive approach. By accurately identifying discrepancies, maintaining professionalism, seeking collaboration, documenting the resolution process, and upholding confidentiality, a skilled loan signing agent can ensure a smooth and successful signing experience for all parties involved.

Managing and Building a Positive Reputation

Effectively managing and building a positive reputation is a critical component of a successful career as a loan signing agent. Your reputation not only impacts your credibility but also plays a significant role in attracting new clients and opportunities. In this section, we will explore strategies to effectively manage and cultivate a positive reputation in the industry.

Consistency in providing exceptional service is paramount when it comes to building a positive reputation. Every interaction with clients should reflect your commitment to delivering high-quality work. Strive for excellence in every signing transaction, paying meticulous attention to detail. Consistency fosters trust and confidence in your abilities, establishing a solid foundation for a positive reputation.

Maintaining professionalism is essential in all aspects of your work. Treat every client, lender, and industry professional with courtesy and respect. Adhere to ethical standards and best practices, consistently upholding the highest level of professional conduct. Punctuality, responsiveness, and effective communication are key elements of professionalism that contribute to building a positive reputation.

Communication plays a vital role in managing and cultivating a positive reputation. Timely and effective communication is crucial in responding to client inquiries, addressing concerns, and providing updates. Clear and concise communication helps build trust and establishes you as a reliable and trustworthy professional. Active listening and empathetic communication also contribute to a positive client experience.

Exceptional customer service is a cornerstone of building a positive reputation. Go above and beyond to meet your clients' needs, anticipating their requirements and surpassing their expectations. Actively listen to their concerns and provide timely solutions. By providing a superior customer experience, you create a positive impression and foster long-lasting relationships with your clients.

Continual professional development is vital for maintaining a positive reputation. Stay updated with industry trends, regulations, and best practices. Attend industry conferences, workshops, and training programs to enhance your knowledge and skills. Being knowledgeable and well-informed demonstrates your commitment to delivering the best possible service to your clients, further enhancing your professional reputation.

Client testimonials and referrals are powerful tools for building a positive reputation. Encourage satisfied clients to provide testimonials that highlight their positive experiences working with you. Actively seek referrals as they serve as endorsements of your professionalism and expertise. Displaying client testimonials on your website or social media platforms can bolster your reputation and attract new clients.

Networking and collaboration within the industry are crucial for managing and building a positive reputation. Attend industry events, join professional organizations, and engage in online forums or groups to connect with fellow professionals. Collaborating with peers and industry experts not only expands your knowledge but also helps you build a network of trusted colleagues who can vouch for your professionalism and expertise.

Integrity and ethical practices are fundamental to building and maintaining a positive reputation. Uphold the highest ethical standards in all your dealings with clients, lenders, and other parties involved in the signing process. Prioritize honesty, transparency, and fairness in your interactions. Acting with integrity strengthens your reputation and fosters trust, setting the stage for long-term success in your career.

Establishing a strong online presence and consistent branding contribute significantly to managing and building a positive reputation. Develop a professional website that showcases your services, experience, and client testimonials. Utilize social media platforms to engage with your audience, share industry insights, and demonstrate your expertise. Consistent branding across all platforms reinforces your professional image and strengthens your reputation.

Lastly, embrace a mindset of continuous improvement. Seek feedback from clients and colleagues and use it constructively to enhance your skills and services. Stay open to learning new techniques and technologies that can improve your efficiency and the quality of your work.

Demonstrating a commitment to growth and improvement sets you apart as a professional of great success.

By implementing these strategies, you can establish yourself as a trusted professional and enhance your reputation in the industry.

Maintaining Professionalism

Maintaining professionalism is a cornerstone of success in any career, and as a loan signing agent, it is especially crucial. Professionalism encompasses a range of qualities and behaviors that contribute to a positive reputation and effective client relationships. In this section, we will delve into the importance of maintaining professionalism and explore strategies to uphold professional standards in your role.

First and foremost, professionalism starts with your appearance and demeanor. As a professional in the loan signing industry, you should present yourself in a manner that instills confidence and trust in your clients. Dress in appropriate business attire that reflects the seriousness and importance of the transactions you handle. Maintain good personal grooming and hygiene to convey a polished and professional image. Additionally, approach every interaction with a positive attitude and maintain a calm and composed demeanor, even in challenging situations.

Clear and effective communication is a vital aspect of professionalism. As a loan signing agent, you must communicate with various parties involved in the signing process, including clients, lenders, title companies, and attorneys. Ensure that your communication is prompt, courteous, and professional at all times. Use clear and concise language to convey information, and avoid technical jargon or overly complex terms that may confuse clients. Active listening is also crucial in effective communication. Take the time to understand your clients' needs and concerns, and address them in a respectful and considerate manner.

Maintaining professionalism also means being punctual and respecting deadlines. Time management is essential in the loan signing business, as delays can have significant consequences for all parties involved. Arrive at appointments on time, and if unforeseen circumstances arise, communicate promptly and provide updated timelines. Respect the deadlines set by lenders and other stakeholders, ensuring that all required documents are signed and delivered within the specified timeframe. By honoring commitments and respecting time, you demonstrate reliability and professionalism.

Confidentiality and privacy are critical aspects of professionalism in the loan signing industry. You will have access to sensitive and confidential information during the signing process, including personal financial details of borrowers. It is essential to handle this information with the utmost discretion and respect privacy regulations. Safeguard client information by maintaining secure document storage and employing appropriate data protection measures. By prioritizing confidentiality, you build trust and foster a professional relationship with your clients.

Professionalism also extends to your knowledge and expertise in the field. Stay up to date with industry regulations, changes in loan documents, and best practices. Continually expand your knowledge through professional development opportunities, such as attending workshops, webinars, or industry conferences. By staying informed, you demonstrate your commitment to delivering accurate and reliable services to your clients. Additionally, seek opportunities to acquire certifications or designations that further validate your expertise in the field.

Another crucial aspect of professionalism is the ability to adapt and handle challenging situations with grace and composure. In the loan signing industry, you may encounter difficult clients, complex transactions, or unexpected issues during the signing process. It is essential to remain calm, focused, and professional, even in these challenging circumstances. Maintain a problem-solving mindset, actively seeking solutions and working collaboratively with clients and other stakeholders to overcome obstacles. Your ability to handle difficult situations professionally will not only strengthen your reputation but also contribute to successful outcomes for your clients.

Building and maintaining professional relationships is a fundamental aspect of professionalism. Cultivate positive and respectful relationships with clients, lenders, title companies, and other professionals you interact with. Demonstrate integrity in all your dealings, treating everyone with respect and fairness. Foster open and transparent communication, addressing any concerns or conflicts promptly and professionally. Building strong professional relationships creates a network of support, collaboration, and referrals, further enhancing your professional success.

Lastly, maintaining professionalism involves self-reflection and continuous improvement. Regularly evaluate your performance and seek feedback from clients and colleagues. Embrace constructive criticism as an opportunity to learn and grow. Identify areas where you can enhance your skills or knowledge and take proactive steps to improve. Invest in your professional development by attending training programs, reading industry publications, or participating in professional communities. By demonstrating a commitment to self-improvement, you position yourself as a dedicated and forward-thinking professional.

Maintaining professionalism as a loan signing agent is essential for building a successful and respected career. It encompasses various aspects, including appearance, communication, time management, confidentiality, expertise, adaptability, relationship-building, and continuous improvement. By upholding professional standards in these areas, you not only enhance your own reputation but also contribute to a positive and trustworthy industry image. Strive to be a consummate professional, embodying the values and behaviors that set you apart in the loan signing field.

Communication with Clients

Communication with clients is a cornerstone of success in any business, and as a loan signing agent, it is crucial to develop strong communication skills to effectively interact with your clients.

Building rapport, establishing trust, and providing clear and concise information are key elements of successful client communication. In this section, we will explore strategies for effective communication with clients, focusing on building relationships, providing accurate information, and ensuring clarity in all interactions.

First and foremost, building rapport with your clients is essential to establish a strong foundation for communication. Take the time to get to know your clients on a personal level and show genuine interest in their needs and concerns. Engage in active listening, allowing them to express their thoughts and questions fully. This demonstrates that you value their input and are dedicated to addressing their specific needs. By establishing a personal connection, you create an environment of trust and open communication, setting the stage for a positive and productive relationship.

When communicating with clients, it is crucial to provide accurate and reliable information. As a loan signing agent, you are responsible for guiding clients through the complex process of signing loan documents. Ensure that you are well-informed about the specific details of the loan, the documents involved, and any relevant regulations or requirements. This knowledge enables you to answer clients' questions accurately and address any concerns or uncertainties they may have. By providing accurate information, you instill confidence in your clients and reinforce your role as a trusted professional.

Clarity is another essential aspect of effective client communication. Loan documents can be complex, filled with legal and financial terminology that may be unfamiliar to borrowers. It is your responsibility to explain the documents in a clear and concise manner, using language that is easily understood by your clients. Avoid technical jargon and explain any complex concepts or terms in simple and relatable terms. Break down the information into manageable pieces, ensuring that clients comprehend each step of the signing process. By promoting clarity, you empower clients to make informed decisions and alleviate any anxieties they may have.

Tailoring your communication style to the needs of your clients is also crucial for effective communication. Recognize that clients have different levels of familiarity with the loan signing process and varying comfort levels when it comes to financial matters. Adjust your communication approach accordingly, adapting your language and level of detail to meet each client's specific needs. Some clients may prefer a more thorough explanation, while others may prefer a concise overview. By being flexible and attentive to your clients' preferences, you enhance their understanding and engagement in the process.

In addition to verbal communication, nonverbal cues also play a significant role in client interactions. Pay attention to your body language, tone of voice, and facial expressions when communicating with clients. Maintain a friendly and approachable demeanor, exuding confidence and professionalism. Use eye contact to establish connection and demonstrate your attentiveness. Nonverbal cues can significantly impact how clients perceive and respond to your communication, so strive to project a positive and reassuring image.

Timeliness is a critical aspect of client communication. Responding promptly to client inquiries, emails, and phone calls is essential for maintaining open lines of communication and building trust. Acknowledge receipt of messages and set clear expectations regarding when clients can expect a response. Even if you do not have an immediate answer, let the client know that you are working on their inquiry and will provide a thorough response as soon as possible. Prompt and timely communication reflects your commitment to addressing their needs and fosters a sense of professionalism and reliability.

During the loan signing process, unforeseen issues or challenges may arise. It is important to communicate these issues to clients promptly and effectively. Be transparent and honest about any challenges or delays, offering solutions or alternative options whenever possible. Communicate the steps you are taking to resolve the issue and keep clients informed of the progress. This proactive approach to communication demonstrates your dedication to providing exceptional service and managing any obstacles that may arise.

Finally, always strive to maintain a professional and courteous tone in all client communications. Treat every interaction with respect and professionalism, regardless of the circumstances. Be patient and understanding, particularly if clients express concerns or frustrations. Respond in a calm and composed manner, providing reassurance and addressing their concerns in a constructive manner. By maintaining a professional and courteous demeanor, you create an environment of trust and collaboration, fostering positive and long-lasting client relationships.

Effective communication with clients is a fundamental skill for a successful loan signing agent. Building rapport, providing accurate information, ensuring clarity, adapting to clients' needs, demonstrating professionalism, and being timely and transparent are all key components of effective client communication. By honing these skills and consistently applying them in your interactions, you can cultivate strong relationships, instill confidence, and contribute to the overall success of your loan signing business. Remember, effective communication is not just about conveying information; it is about building connections and creating exceptional experiences for your clients.

Managing Credentials and Errors

Managing credentials and errors is a critical aspect of the loan signing agent profession. As a highly experienced professional, you understand the importance of maintaining accurate and up-to-date credentials while effectively managing any errors or discrepancies that may arise. In this section, we will delve into strategies for managing credentials and handling errors, ensuring that you maintain a high level of professionalism and deliver exceptional service to your clients.

First and foremost, it is crucial to maintain your credentials in an organized and systematic manner. This includes keeping track of your notary commission, certifications, insurance, and any other relevant documentation. Regularly review and update your credentials to ensure that they are current and valid. Set up a system for documenting expiration dates and renewal requirements, and establish reminders to ensure timely renewals. By staying on top of your credentials, you demonstrate your commitment to professionalism and compliance with industry standards.

In the event of an error or discrepancy, it is essential to handle the situation promptly and professionally. Errors can occur for various reasons, including clerical mistakes, miscommunication, or unforeseen circumstances. When an error is identified, take immediate action to rectify the situation. This may involve contacting the appropriate parties, such as the lender, title company, or borrower, to inform them of the error and discuss the necessary steps to correct it. Approach the situation with transparency, honesty, and a problem-solving mindset.

When communicating about errors, it is important to remain calm and composed, even in high-pressure situations. Adopting a solution-oriented approach will help you address the issue effectively and minimize any potential negative impact. Clearly communicate the error to the relevant parties, providing them with a detailed explanation of what went wrong and how you plan to resolve it. Be proactive in proposing solutions and alternatives to mitigate any inconvenience caused by the error. By taking ownership of the situation and demonstrating your commitment to resolving it, you build trust and maintain your professional reputation.

In managing credentials and errors, it is essential to prioritize ongoing professional development. Stay abreast of industry changes, regulations, and best practices through continuous education and participation in relevant workshops, seminars, and conferences. This commitment to professional growth not only enhances your knowledge and skills but also demonstrates your dedication to providing exceptional service to your clients. By continuously improving yourself and staying informed, you position yourself as a trusted expert in the field.

Maintaining accurate and error-free documentation is another critical aspect of managing credentials. When preparing loan documents, pay close attention to detail, ensuring that all information is accurate, complete, and properly executed. Double-check dates, names, and other pertinent details to minimize the likelihood of errors. Develop a systematic process for reviewing and verifying documents before and after the signing appointment. By exercising diligence in documentation management, you reduce the risk of errors and ensure compliance with legal and regulatory requirements.

Technology can be a valuable asset in managing credentials and minimizing errors. Utilize digital tools and software to streamline your record-keeping processes. This may include using document management systems, password-protected cloud storage, or task management applications. These tools can help you stay organized, track deadlines, and maintain accurate records of your credentials and documentation. However, it is important to prioritize security and confidentiality when adopting digital solutions. Implement robust security measures to safeguard client information and protect against potential data breaches.

As a seasoned professional, it is crucial to maintain a proactive and preventive mindset when managing credentials and errors. Regularly conduct internal audits and reviews of your processes to identify areas for improvement and potential vulnerabilities. Implement quality control measures to minimize the occurrence of errors and maximize accuracy. This may involve implementing checklists, peer reviews, or other mechanisms to ensure thoroughness and accuracy in your work. By investing time and effort in preventative measures, you mitigate the risk of errors and enhance the overall quality of your services.

Managing credentials and errors is an integral part of being a successful loan signing agent. By maintaining organized and up-to-date credentials, promptly addressing errors, prioritizing ongoing professional development, and utilizing technology effectively, you demonstrate your commitment to professionalism, accuracy, and exceptional service. Remember to approach errors with a problem-solving mindset, communicate transparently, and take proactive measures to prevent future occurrences. By consistently implementing these strategies, you can build a strong reputation, instill confidence in your clients, and thrive in the loan signing industry.

Tips for effectively managing daily signing situations and building a positive reputation

Successfully managing daily signing situations and building a positive reputation as a loan signing agent requires a combination of professionalism, expertise, and exceptional service. Here are some valuable tips to help you navigate daily signing situations and establish a strong reputation for your business:

1. Preparation is Key:

Before each signing appointment, thoroughly review the documents and familiarize yourself with the specific requirements of the transaction. This preparation will allow you to confidently guide borrowers through the process, answer their questions, and address any concerns that may arise.

2. Maintain Clear and Timely Communication:

Effective communication is crucial in ensuring a smooth signing experience. Be proactive in providing updates to all parties involved, including borrowers, lenders, and title companies. Respond promptly to inquiries and address any issues or concerns in a professional and timely manner.

3. Exude Professionalism:

Present yourself in a polished and professional manner during every signing appointment. Dress appropriately, arrive on time, and conduct yourself with confidence and courtesy. Remember, your demeanor and appearance contribute to the overall impression of your professionalism and reliability.

4. Foster Trust and Confidentiality:

Treat all client information with the utmost confidentiality and respect. Emphasize the importance of privacy and assure borrowers that their personal and financial details will remain secure. By fostering trust and maintaining strict confidentiality, you build strong relationships and a positive reputation.

5. Adapt to Different Situations:

Every signing situation is unique, and it's essential to adapt your approach accordingly. Be sensitive to the needs and preferences of borrowers, such as language barriers or disabilities, and make necessary accommodations to ensure a comfortable and inclusive experience.

6. Handle Challenges with Grace:

In the face of unexpected challenges or difficult signers, maintain composure and professionalism. Exercise patience, active listening, and problem-solving skills to find effective solutions. Your ability to handle challenges with grace and professionalism will impress clients and contribute to your reputation.

7. Continuously Improve Your Knowledge:

Stay updated with the latest industry trends, regulations, and best practices. Engage in ongoing professional development by attending seminars, webinars, and training programs. By continuously expanding your knowledge and skills, you demonstrate your commitment to providing the highest level of service to clients.

8. Seek Feedback and Learn from Mistakes:

Request feedback from clients after each signing appointment to gauge their satisfaction and identify areas for improvement. Embrace constructive criticism and learn from any mistakes or shortcomings. Taking proactive measures to address concerns and enhance your performance will contribute to building a positive reputation.

9. Leverage Technology:

Embrace technological tools and software that streamline your workflow and enhance efficiency. Utilize electronic document management systems, digital signature platforms, and secure communication channels to simplify processes and provide a seamless signing experience for clients.

10. Cultivate a Network of Referrals:

Actively engage in networking activities and develop relationships with professionals in related fields, such as real estate agents, mortgage brokers, and attorneys. By nurturing a network of referrals, you expand your reach and attract new clients who value your expertise and professionalism.

By adhering to these tips and consistently providing exceptional service, you can establish a thriving business and become a trusted partner in the loan signing industry.

Chapter 6

Scaling Your Notary Business

Are you a notary business owner looking to take your business to the next level? Scaling your notary business can be exciting and profitable, but it takes more than hard work and ambition. This chapter explores critical strategies for expanding your business, including hiring additional loan signing agents, leveraging technology and automation, broadening your service areas, and even becoming a remote online notary. With these tips, you'll be well on your way to growing a successful notary enterprise that stands out.

Scaling a notary business involves taking strategic steps to grow and expand your operations to reach a larger client base and increase your revenue. As you gain experience and establish a solid foundation, it's natural to seek opportunities for growth and maximize the potential of your notary business. In this section, we will explore various strategies and considerations for scaling your notary business effectively.

1. Streamline Your Processes:

Efficiency is key when scaling any business. Evaluate your current notary processes and identify areas where you can streamline operations. This could involve adopting digital tools and technologies to automate administrative tasks, such as scheduling appointments, managing documents, and invoicing clients. By reducing manual work and increasing efficiency, you can save time and resources, allowing you to take on more clients and expand your business.

2. Build a Strong Online Presence:

In today's digital age, having a strong online presence is crucial for scaling your notary business. Create a professional website that showcases your services, testimonials from satisfied clients, and your contact information. Optimize your website for search engines to increase your visibility in online searches. Additionally, establish a presence on social media platforms, such as LinkedIn,

Facebook, and Instagram, to connect with potential clients and build relationships in the industry.

3. Expand Your Service Offerings:

To attract a broader client base and increase your revenue streams, consider expanding your service offerings beyond traditional notary services. You could explore providing additional services such as mobile notary services, remote online notarizations (RON), or specialized notarizations for specific industries like real estate or healthcare. By diversifying your services, you can cater to a wider range of clients and tap into new revenue streams.

4. Develop Strategic Partnerships:

Collaborating with other professionals and businesses in related industries can be a powerful strategy for scaling your notary business. Build relationships with real estate agents, loan officers, attorneys, and other professionals who frequently require notary services. Offer them competitive referral commissions or incentives to refer clients to your business. Additionally, consider partnering with signing services or title companies to expand your reach and gain access to a larger client pool.

5. Hire and Train Assistants:

As your business grows, you may find it necessary to hire assistants or employees to help manage the increased workload. Look for individuals with strong organizational skills and attention to detail who can assist with scheduling, document management, and client communication. Provide comprehensive training to ensure consistency in service quality and adherence to legal and ethical requirements. By delegating certain tasks, you can focus on higher-value activities and take on more clients.

6. Invest in Marketing and Advertising:

To attract new clients and increase your visibility, allocate a portion of your budget to marketing and advertising efforts. Consider online advertising platforms like Google Ads or social media ads to target specific demographics and geographic areas. Attend industry conferences and networking events to promote your services and connect with potential clients. Explore local advertising opportunities such as sponsoring community events or partnering with local businesses to reach a wider audience.

7. Monitor and Analyze Key Metrics:

Tracking and analyzing key metrics is essential for scaling your notary business effectively. Monitor metrics such as client acquisition rate, revenue growth, average transaction value, and client retention rate. By understanding these metrics, you can identify areas for improvement, make data-driven decisions, and adjust your strategies accordingly. Regularly evaluate the return on investment (ROI) of your marketing efforts and assess the effectiveness of different growth strategies.

8. Maintain Excellent Customer Service:

As your notary business scales, it's crucial to prioritize exceptional customer service. Word-of-mouth referrals and positive reviews can significantly impact your growth. Ensure that you maintain professionalism, prompt communication, and a friendly demeanor with every client interaction. Strive to exceed expectations and go the extra mile to ensure a smooth and pleasant experience for your clients. A satisfied client is more likely to refer your services to others, contributing to the growth of your business.

9. Stay Abreast of Industry Changes:

The notary industry is constantly evolving, with new regulations, technologies, and best practices emerging. To stay ahead of the curve and continue scaling your business, it's essential to stay informed about industry changes. Join professional organizations, attend industry conferences, and participate in continuing education programs to enhance your skills and knowledge. By staying abreast of industry trends, you can adapt your business strategies accordingly and position yourself as a trusted expert in the field.

10. Seek Feedback and Adapt:

Lastly, as you scale your notary business, actively seek feedback from your clients and make adjustments based on their suggestions. Regularly assess client satisfaction through surveys or follow-up calls. Use this feedback to refine your processes, enhance service quality, and address any areas for improvement. Adaptability is crucial for long-term success, and by incorporating feedback into your business practices, you can continue to meet the evolving needs of your clients.

Scaling your notary business requires careful planning, strategic decision-making, and a commitment to continuous improvement. By streamlining processes, expanding your service offerings, building a strong online presence, developing strategic partnerships, and investing in marketing efforts, you can reach a wider client base and increase your revenue. Remember to prioritize excellent customer service, monitor key metrics, stay informed about industry changes, and adapt your strategies accordingly. With dedication and the right approach, you can successfully scale your notary business and achieve your growth goals.

Hiring Additional Loan Signing Agents

Hiring additional loan signing agents is one of the most effective ways to scale your notary business. By doing so, you can take on more clients and expand your reach without burning yourself out.

The key to successful hiring is finding qualified candidates who share your commitment to excellent customer service. Always hire individuals with a strong work ethic who are precise about details, trained, and experienced in the industry.

Before bringing someone on board, ensure you have a clear plan for training and managing new comments. It will ensure that each team member is on the same page and working according to the program to achieve the goal.

Communication is critical when working with remote or freelance loan signing agents. Make sure you have reliable methods for staying in touch and sharing vital information about assignments as they come up.

With the right approach, hiring additional loan signing agents can be a game-changer for your notary business.

Expanding Your Areas of Service

Expanding your service areas is a great way to grow your notary business. By offering mobile services, you can provide convenience for your clients and increase your credibility and earning potential. Research the demand in neighboring towns and cities to expand your service areas.

Once you have identified potential areas for expansion, you must connect with real estate agents and other professionals in those regions. Attend networking events and introduce yourself as a mobile notary who provides services in their area.

Another great strategy to expand your areas of service is through online marketing. Create a website that highlights the different locations you serve. It will help attract new customers looking for notaries in specific locations.

Additionally, consider partnering with other businesses that offer complementary services, such as mortgage brokers or insurance agencies. These partnerships can lead to referrals and increased visibility within new markets.

Expanding your service areas requires effort, but it's an efficient way to scale up your business while providing valuable services to more people needing notarization assistance.

Leveraging Technology and Automation

As a notary business owner, you can leverage technology and automation to streamline operations, better efficiency, and reduce costs. One option can be using electronic signature software that allows clients to sign documents remotely from anywhere in the world. It guides the need for physical signatures and saves time.

Another way is by implementing digital record-keeping systems that allow you to store client information securely online. You can also use scheduling tools that integrate with your calendar to book appointments without manual input automatically.

Technology can also help you market your services more effectively. For example, creating a website that showcases your business and its services can attract new clients. Social media platforms like LinkedIn are another avenue for marketing through reaching out to prospects directly or sharing relevant content about your industry.

Leveraging technology and automation has many benefits for scaling up your notary business while reducing operational costs simultaneously, making it easier for potential customers to find you online, and simplifying processes on both ends of transactions to provide an excellent customer experience all around.

Becoming a Remote Online Notary

Becoming a Remote Online Notary (RON) is an exciting opportunity for notaries to expand their services and adapt to the digital age. RON allows notaries to perform notarial acts remotely, utilizing technology to verify identities, authenticate documents, and conduct signings virtually. This innovative approach offers convenience, efficiency, and accessibility for clients, while still upholding the necessary legal requirements and safeguards. Here are key aspects to consider when becoming a Remote Online Notary:

1. Understanding the Legal Framework:

Familiarize yourself with the legal requirements and regulations governing RON in your jurisdiction. Each jurisdiction may have specific rules and guidelines that you must follow to operate as a Remote Online Notary. Consult the relevant statutes, administrative rules, and guidance issued by your state or country to ensure compliance.

2. Meeting the Eligibility Criteria:

Determine the eligibility criteria to become a Remote Online Notary. This may include being a commissioned notary public, completing additional training or certifications specific to RON, and meeting any technology or equipment requirements mandated by your jurisdiction. Ensure that you meet all the prerequisites before pursuing a career as a Remote Online Notary.

3. Obtaining the Necessary Technology:

As a Remote Online Notary, you'll need access to the appropriate technology and tools to perform virtual notarizations effectively. This may include a reliable internet connection, a computer or mobile device with a camera and microphone, secure digital document platforms, and electronic signature software. Invest in the necessary technology to ensure smooth and secure remote notarization sessions.

4. Engaging in Training and Education:

Participate in comprehensive training programs and educational resources focused on Remote Online Notarization. These programs can help you understand the technical aspects of conducting remote notarizations, familiarize you with the available software and platforms, and provide guidance on best practices for maintaining security and compliance.

5. Establishing Secure Procedures:

Develop robust procedures and protocols to ensure the security and integrity of remote notarizations. This includes verifying the identity of signers through knowledge-based authentication questions, credential analysis, or other approved methods. Implement strict security measures to protect the integrity of the notarial act and the privacy of client information.

6. Adapting Notarial Acts to the Digital Environment:

Understand how traditional notarial acts can be adapted to the remote environment. Determine the specific types of documents that can be notarized remotely, such as acknowledgments, jurats, or other authorized notarial acts. Ensure that you are familiar with any additional requirements, such as audio-video recording, recordkeeping, and retention obligations.

7. Offering Convenience and Accessibility:

Highlight the convenience and accessibility of remote notarization services to attract clients. Emphasize the time and cost savings, especially for clients who may be located in different geographical areas or have limited mobility. Market your services to individuals, businesses, and industries that can benefit from the convenience and efficiency of remote notarizations.

8. Building Trust and Reputation:

Establishing trust is crucial in the notary profession, and this holds true for Remote Online Notaries as well. Prioritize professionalism, accuracy, and exceptional customer service in every interaction. Implement robust security measures, maintain strict confidentiality, and adhere to legal and ethical standards to build a strong reputation as a reliable and trustworthy Remote Online Notary.

9. Staying Updated on Regulatory Changes:

The field of Remote Online Notarization is evolving rapidly, with new laws, regulations, and technology emerging. Stay informed about the latest updates and changes in your jurisdiction. Join professional organizations and engage with industry experts to stay up-to-date on industry trends, participate in discussions, and advocate for the advancement of Remote Online Notarization.

10. Collaborating with Industry Stakeholders:

Collaborate with industry stakeholders, such as title companies, lenders, real estate professionals, and legal professionals, to promote the use of remote notarizations. Educate them on the benefits and legality of remote notarizations, and explore opportunities for partnerships and referrals. Position yourself as a trusted expert in the field to attract more clients and expand your business.

By offering convenience, building trust, and staying updated on regulatory changes, you can establish a thriving career as a Remote Online Notary and contribute to the advancement of the notarial profession.

Notary Business Expansion Strategies

Expanding your notary business is a great way to increase profits and reach new customers. But as with any business expansion, it's essential to have a solid strategy in place.

One approach to expansion is through strategic partnerships. Consider partnering with real estate agents or mortgage brokers who can refer clients needing notary services. Another option is to join networking groups or attend industry events where you can make connections and build relationships.

Another key element of expanding your notary business is marketing. The grown social media platforms such as Instagram, Facebook, and LinkedIn can promote your services and share customer testimonials. Consider creating a website that highlights the benefits of working with your company.

It's also essential to continuously improve the quality of your services by investing in training and education for yourself and any additional staff members you may hire.

Be open-minded when considering different avenues for growth opportunities. Feel free to experiment with new services or markets if there is demand for them within your target audience.

Expanding your notary business may seem daunting initially, but it can lead to great success with the right strategies and mindset. Hiring additional loan signing agents, developing your service areas, leveraging technology and automation, and becoming a remote online notary are all effective ways to scale your business.

Remember that growth requires patience and persistence. Take the time to analyze your current strengths and weaknesses before deciding which expansion strategy will work best for you. Continuously re-evaluate and adjust as needed based on feedback from clients and employees.

By implementing these proven tactics for scaling a notary business, you can unlock new opportunities for success in this growing industry.

Expanding your notary business involves implementing strategies to grow your client base, increase revenue streams, and establish a stronger presence in the industry. As you seek to expand your business, consider the following strategies:

1. Geographic Expansion:

One of the most common ways to expand a notary business is by targeting new geographic areas. Assess nearby cities or regions that have a demand for notary services but are currently underserved. Research the local laws and regulations pertaining to notary services in those areas and ensure that you comply with any licensing requirements. Establish a presence in these new markets by networking with local professionals, advertising your services, and leveraging online platforms to reach potential clients in the target areas.

2. Diversify Client Base:

Expanding your client base is essential for business growth. Look beyond your current clientele and identify new target markets that can benefit from notary services. For example, you can focus on providing services to real estate professionals, law firms, healthcare facilities, or financial institutions. Tailor your marketing efforts and service offerings to cater to the specific needs of these industries. Building relationships with professionals in these sectors can lead to a steady stream of referrals and recurring business.

3. Offer Mobile Notary Services:

Mobile notary services can be a valuable expansion strategy. Many clients, especially those with busy schedules or limited mobility, prefer the convenience of a notary who can travel to their location. Promote your mobile notary services to individuals and businesses that require on-site notarizations. This can include real estate agents, loan officers, senior living facilities, and corporate offices. Advertise your mobile services on your website, social media platforms, and local business directories to attract clients seeking this convenience.

4. Embrace Remote Online Notarization (RON):

With the rise of digital technologies, remote online notarization (RON) has become an increasingly popular option. RON allows you to conduct notarizations remotely through secure video conferencing platforms, eliminating the need for physical presence. If your jurisdiction permits RON, consider expanding your services to include online notarizations. This can attract clients who prefer the convenience and speed of remote notarizations, particularly for documents that don't require physical signatures. Familiarize yourself with the legal requirements and technology platforms associated with RON to offer this service effectively.

5. Develop Specialized Notary Services:

Another way to expand your notary business is by developing specialized services that cater to specific industries or document types. For instance, you can specialize in loan signings, becoming a trusted agent for mortgage lenders or signing services. Alternatively, you can focus on notarizing legal documents, medical forms, or international documents that require additional certifications. Specializing in niche areas can differentiate your business and position you as an expert in those specific fields.

6. Collaborate with Other Professionals:

Establishing strategic partnerships with professionals in related fields can lead to mutual business growth. Reach out to real estate agents, mortgage brokers, attorneys, and other professionals who frequently require notary services. Offer them competitive referral commissions and educate them about the value of working with a reliable notary public. Cultivating these relationships can generate a steady stream of referrals and increase your visibility within the industry.

7. Invest in Marketing and Advertising:

To expand your notary business, invest in targeted marketing and advertising efforts. Develop a comprehensive marketing strategy that encompasses both online and offline channels. Utilize search engine optimization (SEO) techniques to improve your website's visibility in search results. Create engaging content on your website and social media platforms to demonstrate your expertise and attract potential clients. Consider paid advertising options such as Google Ads, social media ads, or local print media to reach a wider audience.

8. Enhance Your Online Presence:

In today's digital age, having a strong online presence is crucial for business expansion. Ensure that your website is user-friendly, informative, and visually appealing. Optimize your website for search engines by incorporating relevant keywords and maintaining fresh and updated content. Actively engage with your audience on social media platforms, responding to comments and inquiries promptly. Encourage clients to leave reviews and testimonials online, as positive feedback can build trust and attract new clients.

9. Acquire Notary Signing Agent Certification:

If you're interested in expanding your notary business into loan signings, consider obtaining a notary signing agent certification. This certification demonstrates your expertise in handling loan documents and increases your credibility among lenders and signing services. Certification programs are available through various organizations, and completing one can open doors to new opportunities in the mortgage industry.

10. Continuously Improve and Adapt:

As you expand your notary business, it's important to continuously improve your skills, adapt to market changes, and stay informed about industry trends. Attend industry conferences, participate in training programs, and join professional organizations to stay updated with the latest developments in the notary field. Seek feedback from clients and incorporate their suggestions into your business practices. By continuously learning and adapting, you can position your business for long-term success and sustained growth.

In conclusion, expanding your notary business requires a combination of strategic planning, targeted marketing, diversification of services, and adapting to industry trends. By considering geographic expansion, diversifying your client base, offering mobile and online notary services, developing specialized services, collaborating with professionals, investing in marketing, and enhancing your online presence, you can position your business for growth. Remember to continuously improve your skills, stay informed about industry changes, and adapt your strategies accordingly. With determination and the right approach, you can successfully expand your notary business and achieve your growth objectives.

Conclusion

Starting a notary public and loan signing agent business offers numerous benefits, such as flexibility and control over your schedule. As an entrepreneur, you can set your timings and pick the people you want to work with. This flexibility will relax you and allow you to create a work-life balance according to your needs and priorities.

Another benefit of starting a business in this field is the potential for higher income and financial growth. You can charge competitive service fees as a notary public and loan signing agent. You can increase your earning potential with diligent marketing and a solid client base. Additionally, you can handle more extensive and lucrative transactions as your reputation grows.

Independence and self-employment are critical advantages of starting your notary public and loan signing agent business. When you become your boss, it gives you the freedom to make independent decisions and shape the direction of your business. You are responsible for your success and have the opportunity to build a brand and reputation that reflects your values and professionalism.

Starting a notary public and loan signing agent business allows you to provide valuable services to needy clients. Your role as a notary public ensures the authenticity and legality of essential documents, which is crucial for various transactions, such as real estate deals, wills, powers of attorney, and loan signings. By offering your services, you contribute to the smooth operation of legal and financial processes, providing peace of mind to individuals and businesses.

This guide assists aspiring entrepreneurs in the notary public and loan signing agent field. It is a comprehensive resource, providing valuable information and guidance on various aspects of starting and running a business in this industry. Following the steps and recommendations outlined in this guide, individuals can navigate the legal requirements, set up their businesses effectively, market their services, overcome challenges, and access relevant resources and support.

In closing, " Notary Public & Loan Signing Agent Business" has provided you with the tools, knowledge, and guidance to embark on a successful journey as a notary public and loan signing agent. We've explored the ins and outs of the industry, from understanding the role of a notary public to mastering the art of loan signings.

Throughout this book, you've gained insights from seasoned professionals who have shared their insider tips, tricks, and strategies. You've learned how to establish a solid foundation for your business, build a strong client base, and maximize your earning potential. You now possess the necessary skills to handle various types of documents and conduct signings with confidence and precision.

Remember, success in this industry requires dedication, continuous learning, and adaptability. Stay informed about industry trends, regulations, and best practices. Network with other professionals, attend conferences, and seek opportunities for professional development. With each signing you complete, strive to exceed your clients' expectations and deliver exceptional service.

Starting a notary public and loan signing agent business can be a rewarding side hustle or even a full-time venture. The flexibility, income potential, and fulfillment that come with helping people navigate important legal and financial transactions are truly invaluable. By implementing the strategies outlined in this book and remaining committed to your growth, you can turn your passion for notarization and loan signings into a thriving and lucrative business.

Now it's time to take action. Go out there, apply what you've learned, and begin your journey as a successful notary public and loan signing agent. Remember, every signature you notarize and every loan you facilitate brings you one step closer to achieving your financial goals and enjoying the freedom that comes with running your own business.

May this book serve as a constant companion and guide on your path to success. Good luck, and here's to your prosperous notary public and loan signing agent business!

Made in the USA
Coppell, TX
19 August 2023

20539115R00077